KINGDOM MARRIAGE:

What we have learned from ministering to hundreds of couples and our own amazing marriage journey

RODNEY AND KATHY TOLLESON

Copyright © 2016 RODNEY AND KATHY TOLLESON

All rights reserved.

ISBN-13:978-1540569028
ISBN-10: 1540569020

DEDICATION

We want to dedicate this book to all the couples we have worked with who shared their heart aches, their frustrations, their hidden secrets and their disappointments but who chose to stand for their marriage through personal healing, learning new tools, honest communication with us and each other and who did the hard work of change. Congratulations to all of you. We thank you for helping us grow and press into the Lord for deeper revelation, anointing and understanding. We wouldn't be who we are without you in our lives. Each time we see a marriage heal, grow and prosper, we are blessed and we also know because of it, the Kingdom is blessed.

CONTENTS

	Introduction	11
1	Nothing New	13
2	Adversarial Marriages	19
3	Building a Trust Account	25
4	Hearing Hearts	31
5	A Formula for Decision Making	41
6	Help, Your Differences Are Killing Me	47
7	Identifying, Understanding and Ministering to Triggers	53
8	Unpack It	59
9	Leftovers	65
10	SEX: Unafraid and Unashamed	71
11	Cracks in the Foundation	77
12	Marriage Vision	83

ENDORSEMENTS

"At Christian International, we teach and model the 10M's to all our ministers. They include Manhood, Ministry, Message, Maturity, Marriage, Methods, Manners, Money, Morality and Motives. Rodney and Kathy Tolleson have been ordained with our ministry for twenty-five years. Their book, *Kingdom Marriage*, is full of practical and sensible information along with spiritual insight and revelation that has been battle tested. They have proven the principles in their own lives and the lives of people they have ministered to over the years. I highly recommend this book to help good marriages become better and to help put struggling marriages on a new foundation with equipping for ongoing transformation."

- Dr. Bill Hamon, International Speaker, Author & Founder of Christian International

"Insightful, authentic and vulnerable are words that describe Rodney and Kathy Tolleson's latest book on marriage. They share from their own marriage journey real life challenges creating a foundation of trust for the reader. The solid, practical guidelines present a pathway of change and opportunity for increased intimacy in their marriage relationship. Hope is ignited that healing and restoration in marriage is not only possible but available to all who are willing to pursue a Kingdom Marriage. We highly recommend this book to every married couple or for those considering marriage."

- Lee and Cindi Whitman, Executive Directors of Restoring the Foundations Ministry

"Kingdom Marriage is an outstanding book by Rodney and Kathy Tolleson to help us understand God's plans for marriage and to achieve it. This is not only a practical book but has major keys to help heal and move your marriage to new levels. It is a great handbook for counselors as well as a personal reference book for individuals and it's a definite must for pre-marriage counseling. It has great points to discuss, reflect on and prayer over after each chapter which are helpful and will bring healing to many as they wait on the Lord. I have had the privilege to sit in and minister alongside Kathy and the results are always incredible. Her own personal life experiences along with her prophetic gifting have produced essentially rich lasting fruit."

- Apostles Greg & Julie Bailey, Founders, EagleNet Ministries & Christian International Directors Australia/New Zealand

"Kingdom Marriage is a priceless tool for husbands and wives and anyone wanting to gain a deeper revelation of Gods design for marriage. It helps you understand how to obtain the beautiful picture of a kingdom marriage on this Earth and how to demonstrate it to the culture. It also brings new hope for those who have been in hard places with their spouse and to know there is a reward for those that stay together, pressing forward with the Lord to obtain something amazing! Also because we have the pleasure of being their daughter and son-in-law, we have seen first-hand how these tools and their own perseverance have brought them to deep places in their marriage and in relationship with the Lord. They are a wonderful example of a Kingdom marriage that inspires others.

- Pastors Greg & Tara Romeo, Senior Pastors, Kingdom Family Church

"Please let Rodney and Kathy's book take your marriage to a higher level... there isn't a stone left unturned. It speaks to ALL of us."

- Cathy McNeish, Business Owner

FOREWORD

"Being heirs together of the grace of life, that your prayers may not be hindered."
I Peter 3:7

My husband, Tom, and I have been married for over 35 years. We married young, had children young, and went into full time ministry when we were young. We have walked through the challenges of not having enough money to make ends meet, of balancing ministry and family, of coping with the heartbreak of miscarriages, and having a child born with a serious birth defect. We have endured the betrayal of friends and walked through the disappointment of disconnected relationships. We have had our fair share of "fights" when the stress and pressure we were dealing with put us at odds with one another or when one of us got angry or offended at the other. When we first got married, we thought we were so much alike. But as we lived together we found out how very different we actually are.

Through the good times and through the challenging times, we have learned that God's grace and power have provided opportunities for us to become one as He intended. Today, we are more in love than ever before! We are one another's best friend! We love spending time together, whether it is in fulfilling our calling in Christ and doing ministry together, enjoying our growing number of grandchildren and family, or taking those special times aside together for adventure, growth and intimacy. We love being married to each other!

Not everyone picking up this book may feel this is possible for you! You may say, "I have read other books.....we have been through counseling together....we just don't see eye to eye....the damage is already done.....we just have to accept this is as good as it gets." I want to encourage you that there is hope, healing, and life for your marriage through employing the fresh and living principles of God's Word. He is a

God that loves to do miracles and loves to turn things around! It is never too late!

In this book, Rodney and Kathy Tolleson share their own personal journey of healing and dealing with their marriage. Healing is God's part. Dealing is our part. Not only do they provide a hopeful testimony of how God heals individuals from dysfunction, past hurts, and ungodly beliefs, but they share how they have worked with God to transform their marriage into one of partnership, friendship, and emotional honesty. Rodney and Kathy also provide recommendations for additional resources that will enhance effectiveness for specific areas of healing.

Whether you are seeking help for your own marriage or perhaps you are someone who counsels and supports others in their marriages, you will find the truths in this book to be transformation tools for life and ministry. Learning how to approach adversity through wisdom and revelation, the anointing of the Holy Spirit, as well as through doing the hard work of utilizing practical principles will cause you to experience life, love, and laughter on a whole new level.

For those seeking the treasure of a strong, healthy marriage this book will be a gold mine! Thank you Rodney and Kathy for your transparency, wisdom and message of hope!

Jane Hamon
Vision Church at Christian International

INTRODUCTION

We know there are many great books on marriage that have already been written and have read a number of them ourselves, so it took some serious nudging from the Lord before we decided to write *Kingdom Marriage*. Some of the books on marriage share great philosophical and spiritual ideology, but may not provide practical applications that really work; other books have provided us with insight and ideas that have really been helpful. Our goal is to keep it real and share the things we have found that really worked in our own marriage and the marriages we have counseled.

We have been married for over thirty years and also had the challenge of having previous marriages. Normally, that can be a recipe for another disaster. But we can truly say that by allowing the Lord to put our relationship together, and through co-laboring with Him, we've been able to make a good marriage great. Over the years, as pastors, we had the opportunity to minister and counsel hundreds of couples. As apostolic leaders, we also have ministered to heads of ministries and businesses and those in leadership around the world and have discovered that marriage problems in any language and at any stage of life have the same commonalities and carry the same pain and destruction to families. We have learned one thing, there is nothing worse on earth than marital hell. It sucks the joy out of life and family and robs peace and fulfillment. The Kingdom suffers as a result and it defiles our Christian witness.

Out of the combination of our own marriage, along with the lives of those who so bravely stepped up and bared their own heartbreak, difficulties, and marital shame in the ministry room, we wanted to bring an even greater measure of redemption by touching other marriages through the pages of this book. We believe that the anointing is transferable, that faith is tangible, and that the Lord is always eager to minister to those who are on the great spiritual adventure called marriage. Ultimately, we trust that the Holy Spirit will use this book to touch your marriage.

In these pages, we will be sharing spiritual and practical applications that we have seen restore, revive, and heal marriages. Any examples that are used have been adjusted for the sake of privacy. If you feel that you may see yourself or your marriage in anything we share, trust us, there is nothing new under the sun and there were probably a hundred before you with basically the same issues.

At the end of each chapter there is an "Ask Yourself" section. Each one will contain five questions. We encourage you to get a notebook and write down the questions and answers. If you are going through the book at the same time you can share and discuss each section with your spouse. If not, you can save your answers for when your spouse does read the book and then share with each other. These are digestion questions. We can eat food, but if we don't digest it our bodies won't develop. The same thing applies to information, we can do a lot of ingesting, but if we don't take time to really process it on a personal level we won't get the most out of it. If you want to see growth in your marriage, we encourage you to take the time to "Ask Yourself' and spend some time with the Lord as you process your answers. Also, those questions require you to focus on you and not your spouse. That's one of the keys that is so critical in marriage counseling. Until each person begins to really, truly look at himself and start taking responsibility, they just go round and round.

As in any counsel, until principles and instruction are applied nothing really changes. The Word of God is powerful and living, but the Apostle James made it very clear that it takes being doers of the Word, not just hearers only. We pray that your heart will be touched by the Lord and that His Spirit of Counsel, Understanding and Knowledge will rest upon you so that you will not only get information but you will be empowered for transformation.

CHAPTER ONE:
NOTHING NEW

If you spend any length of time discussing issues with couples you will quickly learn that King Solomon had it right in the book of Ecclesiastes, "There is nothing new under the sun." It's rare to find an issue in a marriage that you have never heard before; most marriage problems revolve around communication, past hurts, finances, sex, parenting, priorities, expectations and differences between men and women and different personality types.

The majority of these issues have common roots that produce the fruit found in most marriages. Many of the root systems have been built long before a couple meets, but if those roots don't receive ministry they can produce some pretty toxic fruit. Our goal in *Kingdom Marriage* is to give you some practical and spiritual advice along with some hands on tools.

When people come for ministry they say things like, "We are having trouble in our marriage or we want to come and get help with our marriage," like it is some kind of third party. If they could just drop it off at the office without being there, they would probably like that. "We are making an appointment to bring our marriage by at 2:00 pm for you to fix it and will be back at 4:00 pm to pick up. We hope that you will have it in better shape because we are really unhappy with it." Just being facetious but you get the picture.

It's important that we establish up front that your marriage is comprised of "you" and "you." It is the two of you together. It is each of you having issues that are creating the problems in the marriage relationship. The marriage only brought about enough intimacy and rubbing together to cause your unresolved issues to surface. The Bible says, "the wounds of a friend are faithful," (Proverbs 27:6) and often times they are faithful to help us discover our deeper wounds. Marriage is a perfect tool for helping us find those places where we need to be healed, transformed, and set free. But if we don't understand that, we resist the process or run from it completely. So as you read this book focus on the "you" part of it. We are most empowered when we accept our own personal responsibility and condition and stop blame shifting our reactions onto others. That is a truth that will set you free not only in marriage, but every area of your life.

Shame Based Relationships

Shame and blame shifting entered into the very first human covenant relationship in the Garden. In Genesis Chapter 3, when Eve decided to eat off of the forbidden Tree of the Knowledge of Good and Evil and then share it with Adam, it opened the door. They both recognized their nakedness and shame set in causing them separation with God. They both got afraid and tried to hide themselves. Part of that fear caused Adam to blame Eve and Eve to blame the serpent. Those fallen sin patterns have to be recognized and crucified in all of us. Many couples don't experience true intimacy because they have too much shame which causes them to use all different types of defense mechanisms to hide their true selves.

Besides blame-shifting for self-protection, they use things like withdrawal, performance, perfectionism, teaching, arguing, anger, silent treatment, addictions, disassociation, etc. The list could go on and on because until we truly allow Jesus to set us free from our shame we continue to fear people really getting to know us. Transparency and vulnerability are impossible when we are still hiding our shame, yet those two items are critical in developing a truly intimate marriage. In Isaiah 61:7, it says that for our shame, Jesus came to give us "double honor." It is part of the gift package of salvation. When we come out of hiding with God and receive His Grace and Forgiveness, it's much easier to come out of hiding with others, especially our spouse. Because if anyone sees our naked areas, it's them!

Getting to Know You

Our whole cultural practice of dating cultivates this problem that then spills over into marriage. When we date, we put our best foot forward and go out and have a good time together. Many times it revolves around activities that don't require any personal intimacy. We encourage courtship prior to marriage (see the Addendum at the end of the book) because courtship begins the whole relationship on a different foundation. It starts with both parties seeking God related to the relationship and then incorporating family and friends. Do you really want to get to know someone? Don't take them to the movies. Spend a work day with them and their family. Do you really want to get to know someone spiritually? Don't go out to eat with them - go to church, to a ministry event or even better yet sign up for a mission trip together. Why missions? It's one of the places where the most pressure can be put on a person, spiritually, physically and emotionally. You don't have the comforts of home, you're not in control, you're confronted by a different culture, language, foods, etc., the schedule and time changes will usually have you with a degree of sleep deprivation and everything is about laying your life down for someone else. It's one of the closest things you can find to bringing a new baby into your home. Those are the kind of things you don't find out by dressing up and going out to dinner.

So in order to truly get to know someone, we have to make sure we see them outside of a controlled environment and we have to communicate. It's important to have a real clear picture of your spouse's childhood experience, sexual experiences and any traumatic events in their lives. Not every detail is important on the sexual experiences, but we have seen countless couples who withheld from their spouse events like sexual abuse, molestation, pornography exposure, masturbation addiction, homosexual contact and other areas of sexual damage. The opposite spouse has often faced years of overreaction, emotional and physical shutdown or avoidance and a variety of other behaviors without any real concept of what is happening. A lot of Christians use, "Well, it's all under the Blood." And that's very true for the sin, but if it is still affecting your behavior, your spouse has a right to know about it. If it's truly under the Blood, you shouldn't have trouble sharing it.

Many couples have shame related to their family experience, their educational experience, or other social experiences. If it's not discussed, the opposite spouse has no clue. Rodney had a great deal of shame related to illiteracy and his educational experience. He is a very bright man, but because he never learned phonetics because sight reading was being taught at the time, and his shyness kept him from ever getting real help, he developed into a man who had built a lot of defense mechanisms to protect that area of his life. It took time, trust and communication for some of the ministry he needed to be set free. As his wife, if I had no knowledge of what was really going on, I could have been angry, impatient, and not a safe place for him. And by a safe place, I don't mean an enabler. He had already had a family, a church, and a school who had allowed him to smile and serve and make it through life. He shares some of his experiences in his two books, *Passivity* and *Finding Rodney*.

It doesn't mean EVERYTHING has to be shared before marriage, but when you really get the concept that marriage means two becoming one, the walls have to come down. My experiences are your experiences and your experiences are my experiences. Your family becomes my family and my family becomes your family. My trauma becomes your trauma and your trauma becomes mine. My emotional and physical health becomes yours and yours become mine. When you look at your spouse and say, "Wow, this is it for the rest of my life!" it will cause you to be proactive and intentional in your marriage. Now, you didn't hear us say, "nagging and controlling." That never works. Rodney was the "Rolaid King" when I worked for him and when we first got married. He internalized his stress and his diet was very traditionally Southern. I knew he needed ministry to change and it would take time. Thirty-one years later, I live with a healthy man who eats a very fresh diet and goes to exercise boot-camp. Miracles do happen! He married a very angry, wounded woman that needed a lot of healing and he really didn't want to live with that all of his life. But through patience, prayer and ministry, I am a very healed, happy woman. We will share more about how those things can happen as we move through the rest of the book.

Partnership, Marital Hell or a True Marriage?

Over and over again as we begin to counsel or interact with couples we find ministry/business/family partnerships rather than true marriages. They live together out of convenience. Children or other responsibilities keep them together, but they have lost the joy of their relationship. Their sex lives have dropped off. They don't really talk anymore and can't remember the last time they really had fun together. Dreams have been broken and hurts and disappointments have piled up. Just like a computer that has crashed the system needs to be restored and the marriage needs to be rebooted. Sometimes you need help doing that. We can offer suggestions and practical tips but sometimes it takes a little more help and we encourage you not to let pride or shame stand in the way, seek some ministry or professional help if it's needed.

Other times we find Christians living in marital hell. Their children are growing up in a war zone. Their faith won't let them get a divorce but their ability to apply faith and spiritual principles to their marriage is too limited to get the job done. They are what we call "Christians living in a heathen marriage." They handle everything without spiritual guidance and are not able to bring the Spirit of God into their home life. They may go to church, but the church is left as they drive out of the parking lot and the last time God participated in their marriage was at the altar on the day of their marriage. Ecclesiastes 4:12b says, "And a threefold cord is not quickly broken." When we don't invite the Lord to stay entwined in the marriage, we become a twofold cord which can be broken much easier. Sometimes we stay two single-fold cords, and that has no power at all. To have a successful *Kingdom Marriage*, we have to learn how to co-labor with the Lord. No matter what condition your marriage is in, there really isn't anything new under the sun and there are answers. The healing power of God is available for both you and your spouse. Spiritual principles do work. The Lord is still on his Throne. There is always hope. God would not ask us to do something and make it impossible. His desire was that man and woman would come together in a covenant spiritual relationship and co-labor with Him. That plan has not changed.

Ask Yourself

1. What are the main issue areas in our marriage relationship?
2. Do I accept responsibility for my actions and reactions in my marriage?
3. What are the areas from my childhood or life prior to marriage where I may still have unresolved shame?
4. What are some of the defense mechanisms that I tend to use regularly?
5. What are areas of my life that shame may keep me from sharing with my spouse?

RODNEY & KATHY TOLLESON

CHAPTER TWO: ADVERSARIAL MARRIAGES

An adversary is an enemy, a rival, an opponent. When a marriage goes bad that's the way people begin to see their spouse. One thing we like to get straight right from the start with couples is that counseling only further arms an adversarial marriage. When a couple is truly adversarial, they will take the things you say, twist them and turn them into weapons to use against each other. Sometimes you wonder why they search out help at all. Some of their unhealthy motivation can be to go to counseling to shut up the other party, to find support for their side of the issues, or they come in hopes that their spouse can be fixed or to prove that they tried everything before bailing out, etc.

Everything is a weapon and a fight to the adversarial couple. It's always about winning or who is right. Dr. Phil calls them "right fighters." They are not solution orientated and are more interested in being right than in being righteous. They come to counseling looking for someone to agree with them. Because adversarial couples are at war, they have to have an army. They are shameless in recruiting family, friends and even, at times, their own children. They love when they can get a pastor/counselor on their side. Their basic intent is to win you over. They will use charm or pull out the victim card so you feel sorry for them. Their justification knows no end. The one thing they won't do is take responsibility for any of their own issues. We make it clear up front that we are on God's side. They will not be able to recruit us so don't bother trying. We make it clear that we are there to help each one of them deal with the issues of their own lives.

One of the hardest tasks of dealing with an adversarial couple is that they cannot let go of the past. It sounds like this, "You said this to me... Well, but last year, you hurt me when you.... But I would have never done that, if you hadn't done... while we were dating." It goes on and on. True forgiveness would mean letting go of their ammunition dump, and when you're at war disarming is scary. Many times they were raised in families where all they saw were adversarial marriages and relationships and anything else is foreign. It's amazing at how many times present day issues can jump from last week to thirty years ago on their honeymoon or fifteen years ago while they were engaged or ten years ago when they had their first baby. Wounds and battles that are not forgiven, healed, and left in the past continue to fester and infect everyday life. Their partner has become the enemy and whenever someone has become the enemy, our true enemy has won.

If there's going to be successful ministry or counseling take place, détente has to be entered into by both parties. Disarmament has to take place. They have to agree that they are going to both work on the ammunition dump of the past and they have to send their armies home. Sometimes that means repenting to children, family members, and friends for trying to recruit them to their side of the fight by maximizing the issues of their spouse and minimizing their own issues.

We start out by requiring couples to lay down their adversarial positions. They have to agree that the objective is not winning, the objective is learning to love along with getting healing and freedom from their own issues. A commitment to disarm is required and they can no longer recruit people to their side of the battle and that if they try it with us at any time, we will call them on it. If they cannot agree to the terms, we've learned it's best not to waste our time.

So how does this apply to you, the reader? First, do you recognize your marriage as being adversarial? If not, that's great, continue reading. But if you do, take the time to repent to the Lord for trying to do marriage in an adversarial atmosphere. Repent to your spouse for being adversarial. Make a commitment to begin the work of dealing with all of the past hurts and issues through forgiveness and healing with the help of the Holy Spirit. We will share more of the "how to's" as we continue. Repent to the Lord, your spouse, and any people that you have recruited into "the fight." Give them the right to call you on it if they feel you are re-entering into that adversarial territory. Make a decision right now that you will no longer be fighting flesh and blood (Ephesians 6:12) and that you will learn how to war against the enemy regarding your marriage relationship.

Maybe you have been trying to help some adversarial marriages and end up frustrated and beat up in the process. We encourage you to take a stand at the beginning and help them shift out of the adversarial mindset right from the start. As soon as you recognize it, address it. Don't beat around the bush, it will save you a lot of time and energy.

You may be in a marriage where you are the only party ready to disarm and move from an adversarial position. It may feel really dangerous to you. You are going to need to work on seeing that the Lord can protect you and fight for you.

We like to use Joshua Chapter 5:13-14. It's an amazing, powerful revelation that Joshua had to fight a battle that was not just natural but spiritual. Because marriage is not just a natural relationship, but spiritual as well, this lesson is something we all need to learn. Joshua was trying to get the man he saw in the spirit with His sword drawn to tell him whose side He was on but the response Joshua received was, "No, but as the Commander of the army of the Lord I have now come." Joshua then fell to the ground and worshiped. His response was, "What does my Lord say to His servant?"

In other words, we need to understand that long before we got involved our Lord was in a war for the heart and soul of our spouse and/or our children. So many times, we position ourselves in prayer as if we have to get the Lord to see our dilemma and get Him on our side so He will fight for us. The spiritual reality is this is His battle and He has recruited us for the fight. Our response needs to be as Joshua's, "Ok Lord, what's my part? What do you want me to do?" When you move into a position of not being adversarial, but joining the Lord in His Battle for your spouse or children, your prayers become more effective. It's easier to keep your heart right. You will have less stress and you will start seeing more results. And most importantly, He will get the glory when the battle is won.

In the counseling room, we like to use a hula hoop to illustrate this concept. As we put it on the floor, we explain that inside the hoop is "holy ground." That is the space where the individual is operating by Kingdom principles with a spiritually right heart. When each party is standing on the same ground, at the same time, WOW, there's real marriage going on and it's wonderful. However, the pattern usually looks like one person in and the other upset and out of the hoop. Then that person makes his way back to holy ground, but in the meantime the other partner is offended and has jumped back out. The person who jumped out had tried to remain in the hoop, but got hurt and impatient because their spouse didn't respond soon enough. It is back and forth, back and forth. Then sometimes there is a stalemate with both parties out of the hoop. If they both stay out at the same time for a long period of time, the spirit of divorce has already entered into the relationship.

In trying to get marriages back on the right track, you have to help them see how important it is for both parties to get on holy ground at the same time. Sometimes you have to start by getting either the husband or wife to see the benefit of planting themselves on "holy ground" until the other party decides to join them. It's great when both parties work at getting in at the same time, but that is not usually the norm. Wish it was. It makes a counselor's or pastor's job much easier!

A visual hula hoop is a good reminder for you to stay on the same ground as the Lord. We recommend purchasing one to keep in your bedroom until it becomes a way of life. The Commander of the Army of the Lord said to Joshua, "Take your sandal off your foot, for the place where you stand is holy." And Joshua did so. Victories are won by standing on holy ground with the Lord.

Ask Yourself

1. Do I view my marriage from an adversarial perspective?
2. How important is it for me to "win" an argument?
3. Whom have I tried to recruit to see my side of our marital difficulties?
4. What past hurts and injuries am I still holding on to?
5. What usually gets me off of "holy ground?"

KINGDOM MARRIAGE

CHAPTER THREE:
BUILDING A TRUST ACCOUNT

Trust is a very difficult concept to put into words, but it is the most critical element in any relationship. It is a critical part of the foundation we need for a healthy marriage. In the *Strong's Concordance* the word "trust" is a Hebrew word, "chacah." When the Bible talks about trusting the Lord that is the word that is used. It means to flee for protection, to confide in, to have hope, to make refuge and to put your trust in. When we trust someone, we put our confidence in them. We believe they are for us and not against us. They become a safe place for us.

Trust creates an atmosphere for transparency, vulnerability, interdependence, and intimacy. In the next chapter, we are going to discuss communication. It's one of the top problems in marriage and it leads to a multitude of other issues. Without trust, communication is guarded, defensive, limited and unproductive.

In a marriage we are either building a trust account or withdrawing from it. We do it in the big things and in the little. Being late might be a small withdrawal but it breaks trust. Saying you will do something and you don't is a trust withdrawal. Unfaithfulness puts you into a deep deficit. Minimizing, justifying, exaggerating, along with a host of other behaviors chip away at the trust account. You would not have a bank account and never make a deposit and then be angry that there was no money in the account. Many couples don't have trust in their relationship because they aren't making any deposits.

One of the first things we have to do to get couples turned around is to get them to be intentional in their marriage. A lot of people just want to wake up in the morning and have a good marriage but they don't do any investing. In fact, often times they are doing more spending than investing. Trust is something we need to do intentionally. There's a great book called *The Speed of Trust*, by Stephen Covey which helps businesses to see how important it is to establish trust with their customers and how to keep it. If it's necessary in business, how much more critical is it in marriage?

Developing Trust

Obviously, there was enough trust established for the two of you to make a decision to marry. So what happened? Where did the wheels come off? Here's what we have found over the years of ministry. The wheels usually came off in infancy and childhood. Let us explain what we mean. Basic trust is established in infancy. Anytime an infant's needs are met, the ability to trust is reinforced. It is really important to know if we marry someone who was neglected as an infant or child because their ability to trust may need healing and restoration. When trust breaks down at the infant stage of development, it really takes the Lord to establish what is lacking. As they begin to establish a trust relationship with Him, it helps them to build a foundation that they can use in other relationships. It gives a greater understanding to the scripture that says, "When my father and mother forsake me, then the Lord will take care of me (Psalm 27:10). It doesn't mean that if you were left on a doorstep the Lord will then show up in your life. It means in any area where you may have been neglected or not received what you were supposed to receive, the Lord will not forsake you. He will either meet it directly or through the Body of Christ.

As a child develops trust, it is very all or nothing. Children are extremely trusting. It's why they might get in a car with a stranger or allow abuse without telling anyone. They have all or nothing trust. They will trust you and trust you until they finally reach the end of their limit. After that, it's very difficult to rebuild the trust. You had your chance and blew it. Many people bring child trust into the marriage. Their trust abilities never matured. It's all or nothing and at the least sign of a violation of trust their account drops to zero. They enter into the marriage with trust for their spouse and then very quickly it dissipates. Or they come in wanting to trust, hoping they can trust, but not really trusting. It's all or nothing and in a lot of marriages, it has become nothing. There is no trust in the relationship. The Bible tells us to put away childish things as we mature. We have to exchange child trust for mature trust.

Here are some of the differences between the two:

Child Trust – When broken almost impossible to restore.

Mature Trust – When broken can give opportunity to restore beginning with repentance and forgiveness.

Child Trust – Naïve and establishes trust too quickly.
Mature Trust – Discerning and uses wisdom as they establish trust.

Child Trust – Small violations can have overreaching consequences and become big trust breakers.
Mature Trust – Puts trust violations into a healthy perspective.

Child Trust – Generalized trust.
Mature Trust – Can distinguish areas that can be trusted even though there may be other areas where trust is not warranted.

Child Trust – Looks for individuals they can trust 100% of the time in 100% of everything.
Mature Trust – Knows that God is the only One we can put 100% trust in.

Child Trust – Will destroy a marriage relationship.
Mature Trust – Keeps a marriage relationship healthy.

Going from child trust to mature trust is easier said than done, but it starts with identifying the problem and then looking at what caused our trust to be damaged in childhood. We will talk further in Chapter 8, *Unpacking Baggage,* on how to renew the mind in order to move from child trust to mature adult trust. And in Chapter 7, *Identifying, Understanding, and Ministering to Triggers*, we will look at a ministry process which can help us walk through healing where trust was damaged as a child.

Trust and Forgiveness

Many people think trust and forgiveness are one in the same, but they are actually two very different elements. Forgiveness is required by the Lord. We are to forgive as He forgives us but trust must be rebuilt. You may forgive someone but they may not be willing to do anything that could rebuild trust. Restitution is a necessary element to rebuilding trust. Sometimes it can be rebuilt quickly and other times because of previous damage a person might have, the rebuilding can take longer. For example, a woman who had a father who abandoned the family when she was young, a step-father who battled alcoholism, and a mother who left her in the care of a number of people because she had to work didn't grow up in the conditions that foster trust. If her trust is violated, it may take her long to rebuild it. The more ministry she receives the easier it will become. If someone was raised with a really good foundation of trusting relationships, trust can often be re-established in a short amount of time.

Here are some areas that can damage trust in children: abandonment, rejection, divorce, broken promises, sexual abuse, physical abuse and abusive discipline, control, selfishness or narcissism in their parents, unfaithfulness by their parents, neglect, lack of appropriate emotional responses, excessive anger, favoritism, excessive teasing, criticism, addictions, and every time their parents and the adults in their lives do not keep their word. These are just some very common ones. Whenever you have any of these in your background, trust may be difficult. These are the kinds of issues that create damage in our root systems that result in toxic fruit in our relationships. Some men don't trust women. Some women don't trust men. And some people believe they can't trust anyone. Again, it takes renewing of the mind and healing.

These trust issues will also play a big part in our ability to trust the Lord. And if we can't trust the one who is called Faithful and True, who can we trust? It has to start there because ultimately, He is the one who helps us to know who we can trust and to what extent. It's the discernment we receive from the Holy Spirit, that sense of unction in our spirit or that check in our spirit that we feel. This helps lead us. Sometimes people can say all the right stuff, but the Holy Spirit may be telling us something else. We have to trust the Lord and His Voice. The Bible says that His sheep know His voice and they won't follow someone else. We need to be connected prophetically to receive from the Lord. We were created to hear His Voice. It may not always be an audible voice, but we can hear Him through His Word, through the thoughts He drops in our minds, through mental images He shows us, through visions and dreams, and through impressions we have. We are supposed to be led forth by our peace and if we don't feel that peace, we shouldn't move forward. A spirit-led marriage is a peaceful, joyful marriage.

Sometimes we hear things like this, "She said she forgave me but now she's checking on me all the time," or "He said he forgave me, but wouldn't give me back all the credit cards." In other words, they want to bundle forgiveness and trust into one package. Again, they are two different elements. Forgiveness is necessary as a starting place if trust is going to be rebuilt, but they are not one in the same. We have a responsibility to press into the Lord for healing when we have trust issues, but the party that offended has a responsibility to make restitution. They have to do the behavior that will help restore it. Using the examples from above; the man who was caught looking at pornography on the internet needs to be okay with protective programs on his phone and computer. He needs to be willing to let her check the history on his electronic devices, give his wife permission to ask questions and hold him accountable, and do it all with a good attitude. That helps restore trust. The wife who has abused credit cards and has a shopping addiction that has created debt for the family has to understand that she can be forgiven but that doesn't mean a Visa, MasterCard, American Express and Discover card in her wallet. No, trust has to be rebuilt and safeguards need to be put in place. As she and her husband do that together eventually trust can be re-established. When we have violated the trust in our marriage, we have to take responsibility to help re-establish it and it's important to do it intentionally.

There are instances when in helping marriages through the healing and restoration process that we have to go back to times where trust was violated. Sometimes it might be a thirty-year marriage and it goes back to where she felt pressured into sex prior to the wedding. Yes, she has to forgive herself for not enforcing her boundaries but it has to be recognized as the place where trust was first broken. It is like a thorn or sliver that gets in deep and always creates a sense of irritation and pain, especially when pressed. It's important that as a couple you look for those areas and have a real conversation with each other, one where you hear each other's hearts and there is true forgiveness. Again, depending on the condition of the marriage sometimes we can work through those areas on our own, other times it takes getting some outside help. When you start getting down to the basics, you will probably be surprised with how many issues you have in your marriage that are related to trust.

In a Kingdom Marriage, trust in the Lord comes first. Then we allow the Lord to heal areas of our lives that were damaged by authorities and others in our life who violated our trust. We look at our marriage through the eyes of trust. What are the things I can do that will help my spouse trust me? What are the things I do that damage their trust? It's never too late to begin to invest in your trust account.

1. What happened to me as a child that would have damaged my ability to trust? Who did I trust the most as a child?
2. If I rated my ability to trust my spouse from 1-10 what number would I give myself? (1 being the lowest ability and 10 being the highest.)
3. What number would I give my spouse related to their ability to trust me?
4. What are some of the small ways I make withdrawals on the trust account with my spouse?
5. What are some things that I have done that have created large withdrawals on my marriage trust account?

CHAPTER FOUR: HEARING HEARTS

Communication needs its own chapter even though it actually is woven throughout most of the topics within the book. Without communication none of the other stuff works, and without trust it's difficult to have intimate communication. It never ceases to surprise us how much stuff couples have never talked about, or all the things they just don't talk about, and how little time they set aside to really talk. And then they wonder why their marriage ship is off course.

The reason we called this Chapter, *Hearing Hearts,* is because a lot of couples talk to each other but it's a surface conversation. They never really share their hearts or hear what the other person's heart is really saying. A wife can say, "Do I look fat in this?" and if her husband doesn't hear her heart saying, "Am I still attractive to you?" he could get in trouble. A man can spend more and more time at work or the office saying that he's needed there and his heart can really be saying, "I am more respected and feel more needed at work than at home." Part of honest heart communication takes getting in touch with our own hearts and learning to communicate what is really going on inside. Sometimes we can project anger at our spouse, but deep down we are really mad at ourselves. It's also important that we work at really sharing our hearts. For example, you can say, "You're too busy," which could provoke defensiveness or justification. Or you could say, "I miss you and would really like more time together," which will create a very different response.

When we get married, it's often with the distorted concept that our spouse is a mind reader. They should know what we are thinking and feeling. NEWSFLASH – they don't! We have to communicate. If you really wanted something personal for Christmas, communicate or you could end up with a microwave. If something really bothers you every time they do it, communicate or they will keep crunching ice when it drives you crazy. We'll be talking more about sex in the marriage in a later chapter, but the bedroom is another place where communication is critical. We can't tell you how many times we've heard, "I hate when he does such and such." Or, "I know that she's not really there when we have sex." The question is, "Have you told him/her?" The majority of the time the response is, "No".

Most couples do hunger for emotional honesty and intimacy, they just don't know it. They replace the healthy kind with arguing and fighting. An example would be people who are hungry because they need vitamins, minerals and protein, but they replace it with sugar, carbs and starch. It may satisfy, but it's just not good for you. Replacing true intimate communication with strife, isn't a healthy replacement. Usually, when a couple finally gets mad enough, they get honest, except at that level its usually honesty that hurts. If a couple is arguing, we know there's still hope because they are still communicating. When they've stopped any communication, then there's real trouble. If we can get a couple to understand that arguing and strife is just a dysfunctional way of sharing at a more intimate level, we can begin to teach them how to establish healthier, emotionally honest conversation.

What Is Love to You?

One of the basics we like to start off when teaching heart communication is, "What is love to you?" Communicate the answer to that question to your spouse in practical easy-to-do terms. A lot of times we want to love people and give them what we want and need. Think about it, how many times do you gravitate to gifts that you would really want? And unless you stop yourself and put yourself in the other person's shoes, they will be receiving your favorite artwork for their birthday. We often base love on our childhood experiences. Love in our family was camping, boating, and enjoying the outdoors. Rodney finally got it fully on my (Kathy's) 60th birthday. We went hiking that day on the Appalachian Trail. He gave me the smell of the woods, a waterfall, some great exercise, wildlife, and the joy of experiencing nature. For me, it was much more fulfilling than dinner in the fanciest restaurant in town. What really communicates love to you? If you don't know, how will someone else figure it out? It's one of the things that we like to do in pre-marital counseling. We have the couple get in touch and communicate to their fiancé what demonstrable acts of love would look like to them. It takes love from infatuation, attraction, and a generalized feeling to the revelation that just telling a person you love them isn't enough. Undemonstrated love is not love at all. God didn't just tell us He loved us; He gave us His only begotten son as a sacrifice for our sins.

Roadblocks to Communication

In this next section we are going to discuss some of the roadblocks to communication that we come across on a regular basis. They have to be addressed and removed if communication is going to flow freely. Anger and withdrawal are often major factors. They are both emotional overreactions but at opposite ends of the spectrum. If you try to have an honest conversation with your spouse and are met with anger, you will begin to think twice the next time you open your mouth. If you really want communication in your marriage, you have to deal with your personal anger issues or it's like throwing a bucket of cold water on a fire that you want burning. It doesn't work. Withdrawing and going into shut down mode works the same way. It is a self-defensive maneuver usually learned in childhood. Anger and withdrawal may have helped you survive your childhood but it won't help you thrive in life and marriage.

Another communication killer is defensiveness. It's a self-protection mechanism that doesn't allow communication to flow freely. When our spouse tries to speak into our life and we get defensive, it blocks further discussion. Putting up walls or counterattacking along with simply defending before really hearing our spouse causes them to eventually just give up. Most of the time if someone has a problem with being defensive, the root system producing that fruit lies in wounding from childhood. They may have felt attacked, rejected, or unprotected. If they don't work through those deeper issues, true communication will continue to be sabotaged.

Justification is also a deal breaker when it comes to healthy communication. As long as we are trying to justify our behavior and our position, we aren't really able to hear or receive feedback. Part of good communication is being able to hear and see from another person's perspective. Justifying our reactions is not really owning our behavior. If you justify your anger by blaming it on the other person's behavior, you have no power to change. Your spouse is in control of your behavior and emotions. That can be scary. We are empowered when we accept responsibility for our emotions, behavior, and the consequences because it gives us the ability to change it all.

Interrupting is another roadblock to communication. It's especially a problem when you have a contemplator, who has to think a little bit before responding and a partner who is more emotionally impulsive. They usually interrupt the contemplator before they ever get a word out. If you want to have good communication, you have to stop and listen. And you have to listen with your heart. If you're already thinking about what you're going to say next, you're not really listening.

Disconnecting or disassociation while in conversation is also a major roadblock. It is a coping mechanism learned in childhood as a response to stress, strife and trauma. For self-protection, the brain learns to check out of the immediate situation. When this has become a pattern that again helped with survival, it can be difficult to break. And though it may have helped you to survive in childhood, it doesn't help you thrive in a marriage. It takes retraining the brain to focus and concentrate. Women get tired of trying to have a conversation with a guy whose watching sports at the same time and men get tired of women being distracted by kids and being somewhere totally different in their minds. It's so important that we are present if we are going to have good healthy communication. It's important we make space for it by making sure we have communication times where electronics, children and any other distractions are removed (even Fido).

Overreaction is also a deal breaker when it comes to communication. When a spouse knows their partner is going to overreact, they tend to avoid communicating certain things. Let's face it, people avoid discomfort and when we overreact it causes people to feel uncomfortable. If someone starts either crying, yelling, banging things, venting, saying how terrible they are or glaring at you, it wouldn't create an atmosphere conducive for communication. So why do you do it? Are you overreacting because of fear? Are you overreacting because you're hurt? Are you overreacting because you feel blamed? Are you overreacting because you want to shut down the communication? Are you overreacting because you're feeling guilty? Are you overreacting because you don't want to admit you're wrong? We could go on, but again, the overreaction is fruit. What is the heart root of that behavior? That's why it's so important to have a relationship with the Holy Spirit, because what we don't know and understand even about ourselves, He does and has the answer. He can help you get in touch with the real reason you overreact. The majority of time it's because the behavior was modeled by adults in their childhood, or learned has a survival skill. It's immature and healing needs to take place in order to have mature conversations.

You get the point, there are a lot of roadblocks that can crop up due to our own emotional and personal issues. It takes healing and truth in the inward parts to get in touch with the roadblocks we may be using and why we use them. In order to begin establishing real communication in marriage, each party has to make a commitment that the relationship is important enough to lay down mechanisms they have used for years as self-preservation.

Marriage is for Adults

A real important tool for adjusting communication in couples is the understanding of the three basic types of communication. First, we will discuss them and then we will talk about how they play out in marriage. The three different types are Parent, Child and Adult.

When we communicate out of the Parent, we direct, instruct, correct, train, adjust, admonish, discipline, know what's right for the other person, make decisions for the other person, speak for the other person, etc. You get the picture; it's what parents do. It's their job. They will also use facial expressions, looks, and sounds to emphasize the communication. The only problem is that it works with children, but it won't work with your spouse.

The next area we can communicate from is Child. The child will blame shift, minimize, lie, become passive aggressive, mumble, argue, whine, pout, stomp out of a room, get angry, feel picked on, roll their eyes, use body language to communicate, are not able to speak up at times, etc. These are all responses we can see in children, especially if they are feeling overpowered. Again, doesn't make for healthy communication in a marriage.

Adults communicate by respecting each other's boundaries, opinions, ideas and thoughts. They communicate to share with each other, but not to control the other person. There is more back and forth in adult dialogue. Voice and tone is different than with Parent and Child. Marriage is designed for adults.

Here's what you usually find in a Parent-Parent marriage. They both know they are right, they both want to run the show, and they are constantly bumping heads. This is a marriage that can often end up in divorce because neither is willing to give and they are both strong enough to take care of themselves.

Parent-Child marriages are dysfunctional but they often stay together. One is the Parent, the other responds as a Child. Usually the longer they are married the worse it gets unless they seek help. If the Child starts maturing and starts communicating on a different level, it will rock the marriage boat. With these couples, their sex lives generally diminish because who wants to have sex with their Mama, or their Daddy, or a child? Sometimes they flip-flop and one will be the Parent in one area of life and the other the Child and then the roles will flip when they are in another area.

Child-Child marriages would be comical if they weren't so sad. No one is in charge; they bicker about everything. Decision-making is nearly impossible. I always say they are usually the last ones to leave the church parking lot because no one can decide where to go to lunch. No one ever takes responsibility for anything. It's all about me, mine, and me some more. It may end in divorce if one party reaches out for help and starts maturing enough to make a decision. Until then no one is responsible enough to initiate change.

How does this happen? First of all, modeling plays a major role. If you were raised by parents who never had real adult conversations that you could hear, you think being an adult is being parental. That's not the case, and if you are parental in other relationships eventually people push away from you. Even with your adult children, it's important to learn Adult-Adult communication or you will see them at Christmas and Thanksgiving and not a lot in between. They do not want to be parented if they are healthy. Many times older children who have taken care of younger children become parental before they become adult, and so it's a natural language for them. The progressions should be Child, then Adult, then Parent.

If you spouse says things like, "Stop treating me like a child." Or "Yes, Mom." And, "I have to take care of everything around here." Those are real big clues that there is Parent-Child communication going on in the marriage. Again, it's not the exact words, it's the heart and spirit of the communication. When you watch couples, it's usually pretty easy to tell the dynamics of their marriage. We've seen the light bulbs go off many times in the ministry room when we've put this on the blackboard and they realize that they use one of the above combinations, but then the question is, "How do we change?"

So glad you asked. A simple question to ask yourself is, "Would I say that to another adult?" It's also important to begin to watch your body language, facial expressions, and sounds that communicate parental disapproval or childish upset. We encourage couples to come up with a healthy, fun, agreed upon way to cue each other so if one becomes Parent or Child, the other can remind them. This works if not reacted to defensively and if both parties really want to develop healthy mature communication in the marriage.

Counterbalancing

Counterbalancing affects many areas in marriage, but we are going to discuss it related to communication. You can also look at other ways the principle applies to your marriage. Everything in life seeks balance, so if a couple marries and one person is a bit more of a talker, the other person will probably talk less. The less one talks the more the other talks. They counterbalance each other and by the end of the marriage one of them is a non-stop talker and the other is a silent stump. If it's discipline, one tends to be stricter; the other spouse is mercy incarnate. They spend their marriage counterbalancing each other which helps them end up poles apart and in strife. Spending and saving is another area where counterbalancing often takes place in marriage.

So to begin to stop counterbalancing in marriage, it actually takes doing the opposite behavior. It feels counterintuitive, just like cornering a motorcycle; you actually do not steer into the corner, you steer against it. The saver has to spend a little and the spender has to save a little. The disciplinarian has to lighten up and the mercy minded has to exercise some discipline and consequences. The over-emotional has to apply some thought and logic and the over-logical has to apply some emotion. The quick to decide needs to give things some thought while the contemplator, way past decision making time, needs to take a risk and make a decision more quickly. The talker has to quiet down a bit and the non-talker has to speak up. We know, risky business, but it works.

It's great when both spouses enter in at the same time with opposing behaviors, but it still works if one will take the plunge. Usually fear and control interfere and try to stop the process. It sounds like this, "If I stop saving, we won't have anything." Or maybe, "If I don't show love and mercy, our kids will hate us." Or perhaps this, "One of has to have passion and show emotion or we will just be two robots." Related to communication, "If I don't carry the communication, we will look rude and not engaged." Deal with your justification and then try it. It needs to be implemented for a long enough period of time to evoke change. A one-time spurt won't change lifetime patterns. We encourage you to try opposing counterbalancing measures. They really work and will definitely help your communication and other areas where there is disagreement.

In Chapter Six, *Help! Your Differences Are Killing Me*, we discuss in greater lengths the parts that personality and life language styles play in communication. Those differences are also critical in developing communication that really works. Some personality types are more blunt, others are more flowery, some like few details, others need a lot, etc. As a couple, we have to understand our own style of communication while learning the communication style of our spouse and what they need. For example, if your spouse is a personality type that likes fun and humor, it's important not to shut that down if you have a more serious direct approach to communication. Or if you have a personality that is very easy going and your spouse has a more intense personality, it's important that you don't expect your partner to react with the same intensity. It's also just as important that the spouse with the easygoing personality not shut down their more intense partner.

Communication is an art and one of the most important keys to a healthy marriage. If you really want to work on communication in your marriage, there are some great books, blogs, and YouTube videos that can assist you further. We encourage you to keep working on it because it's something that doesn't just happen. Millions of couples have proven it. It takes work, commitment, knowledge, patience, and love.

1. **Do you try to get in touch with your heart and communicate what You really mean?**
2. **Do I use arguing to finally say what I really want to say? (Be honest.)**
3. **What are some of the roadblocks to communication that you use at times?**
4. **Do you tend to communicate more from Parent/Child/Adult with your spouse?**

5. What are some areas that you and your spouse counterbalance each other? What about related to communication?

CHAPTER FIVE:
A FORMULA FOR DECISION-MAKING

Making decisions big or small affect everyday life and if couples don't have a good formula, there is constant strife. Most parenting issues, financial arguments, and other problem areas revolve around the decision making process. We've discovered that there really is a formula that works. We've applied it for years and have seen it make a huge difference in our lives. Also, whenever we have been able to get a couple to apply it in their own lives, they see a major reduction in strife, resentment and emotional sabotage.

Most couples process DECISIONS by a formula that looks like this:

Different Opinions + Strife = Emotional Witchcraft

With this formula, someone always experiences defeat. Here is a practical example: A husband feels he needs a new truck for work. The wife thinks they need to pay off the car first. Husband says, "I am the head of the house; I am buying a truck." It causes strife and then the wife is not emotionally or spiritually supportive of the decision. The power of agreement which gives us increased power over the enemy is not in place. When the transmission goes bad on the truck he just bought without agreement, she is saying, "See, I told you not to get the truck." Now, she might just be saying it on the inside but it's where she is emotionally. Because there wasn't agreement, there is a certain satisfaction when things don't work out. It releases emotional witchcraft into the decision making process. Another example is the wife makes an important decision related to one of the children without any input from her husband. Her justification is, "After all, I spend more time with them and he doesn't take care of them as much as I do." She is more influenced by what the kids want, so rather than risking seeking his advice, mom decides their fourteen-year-old can go on a vacation with one of their friends. On that trip their daughter is molested. Now, the mom is standing alone, not only dealing with the travesty of what has happened to their daughter, but the blame coming from her husband for not allowing him to have input. He is emotionally saying, "I told you, so, when are you ever going to let me help raise our children?" Messy! Strife makes everything messy, and then emotional witchcraft makes it messier. The reality is both parties lose and if there are children, the whole family loses. To foster spiritual support, it requires and environment intimacy, support, and mutual respect.

Often when you listen to husbands and wives discussing points of contention regardless of the arena, you will hear things like "I think" or "I feel." Decisions are often based on wants, past experiences, and their growing-up family values, which can look extremely different between husbands and wives. One party may use some sort of emotional dominance over the other. Anger, the silent treatment, or withholding sex may all be part of the tactics. Then there is the age old religious move, "I am the man and you will submit to me." Really, even if I'm prophetic and the Lord has given me insight as your wife and helper? Really, even if this is a narcissistic, selfish and immature decision? Really, even if this is financially, emotionally or spiritually abusive? Really, if the only one Bible verse you ever want to apply to your life is, "Wives submit to their husbands in all things?"

1. So to even begin a discussion on a spiritual formula that works, we need to look at the true spiritual role of a wife. We can't look at it through cultural norms, traditions, and past experiences, but from a true understanding of God's original intention. When we look at the fact that woman was taken from Adam to be a counterpart and to demonstrate the image of God, we
2. have to understand what that really means. In Genesis 3:26, we are told that God made man in His own image, male and female He created them. This was before Eve was taken from Adam's side and fashioned into a woman. When God created woman, there were no homes to clean, food to cook, dishes to do or clothes to wash and iron. So if man didn't need a maid, who actually was this helper, this "ezer kenegdo" in the Hebrew? Why was she so important? Why was she separated from man to be rejoined with him to become one again through a covenant relationship?

The enemy has subjugated women through a religious spirit for years. Jesus was one of the first great liberators of women. He interacted with them, healed and delivered them, evangelized them, and gave them place in His ministry. The early church was built with powerful women of God co-laboring with men. This is not a treatise on women and the church, but we encourage you to do some serious study yourself on the subject. Women being relegated to bringing food to after church fellowships and teaching Sunday school or singing in the choir wasn't quite what God had in mind when He took part of His Own Image out of Adam and called her woman.

Let's look at the Hebraic understanding of the word "ezer kenegdo." Over time, through translation it lost a lot of it's full meaning. It has come to describe, for many women, a woman who is just supposed to wait till a man does something and then help him, wait on him, serve him. Her own gifts, talents and vision often lay dormant for fear of usurping or looking like she's not a real true helper.

"Ezer kenegdo" is often translated as a fit helper which can draw up images of someone doing a job and the other person handing them tools, or someone serving another person as they do a job. That translation is actually very inaccurate when you get back to the Hebraic definition. Today we often use the word helpmate, which is an even poorer translation of the English phrase "help meet" which means "fit to" or "equal to." But if you go back to the deeper meaning of the Hebraic word ezer, it comes from two roots, '-z-r which means, "to rescue or to save" and g-z-r which means "to be strong." The text would translate more accurately in English if it was said that God created woman to be a power or strength corresponding to man. Everywhere ezer is used in the Old Testament, it always refers to a strong rescuing force.

Kenegdo means "against or counterpart." It comes from the root "neged" which means in front of, in sight of, or opposite to. So this would be a helper who is strong and powerful, as Adam's equal, and up to the task of co-laboring with him in the earth. Some teachers have said that the overall connotation is that when he is flowing with God and is worthy the ezer kenegdo will be a helper for him, and if not she will be against him. That sounds like a lot of marriages we have seen.

When we were first married, I (Kathy) made a decision to follow "submit to your husband" to the letter of the law and to my own understanding at the time. Over the first few years of our marriage there were times that decision cost us in money, reputation, and our own harmony. With no understanding of the prophetic gifting I had, I would sometimes tell my husband things like, "I think this is a trap, don't do it." His business advisors would tell him he had to do it; the trap would shut in just days and it would cost us. I've said, "It took about a quarter of a million dollars to buy my husband's ear." Now he appreciates my prophetic input. At one point of frustration, he finally said, "OK, just say, 'Thus sayeth the Lord'." But I told him 'no' because that would open me up to the spirit of Jezebel, which I wanted no part of. So at that point we decided that I would give input and then we would pray together. It was the beginning stages of an amazing partnership that has given place for my gifting, allowed us to use the power of agreement, and see God do amazing things.

I will never forget the day Rodney told me, "It was great having a wife who would just submit to everything, but what I really want is partnership." I believe on that day I was able to step into being the true "ezer kenegdo" the Lord always intended me to be. I could bring my strength, power, and gifting to the relationship and could walk in equal authority over the enemy, and even confront my husband in love when he needed it. Partnering with Rodney didn't take away my heart of submission, but it empowered me to bring my gifts, revelation and insight to the table in a whole different way. I had also learned that submitting to love is not hard. Many men complain their wives have a submission problem when their own hearts have a love problem.

Now our decision making formula looks like this:

Prayer + Agreement = Heavenly and Earthly Support

We are spirit-filled believers so our first prayer is in our heavenly language. The Bible says in 1 Corinthians 14:2 that when we pray in tongues we are speaking directly to God. It may be a mystery to us, but not to Him. So we believe it's best to weigh in with God before praying in our own understanding. Before we even start to pray, we lay down any of our own agendas, opinions, thoughts, or feelings. We had come to the place in our own lives that nothing mattered more than walking in the spirt and obedience. Getting our own way had done nothing but bring divorce, strife, financial, and family problems into our lives. We wanted Kingdom in everything. The Kingdom of God is righteousness, peace, and joy in the Holy Spirit. Romans 14:17b. The Message

CHAPTER SIX:
HELP, YOUR DIFFERENCES ARE KILLING ME

Rodney and I are as different as night and day and so we understand from our own lives and from ministering to others that how we handle our differences can make or break a marriage. Early on in our marriage we thought part of our job was to help change the other spouse. I (Kathy) tended to get more stirred up about things and Rodney was always trying to bring peace and calm to the world. One day I turned to him (and this wasn't a compliment at the time) and said, "If you had been an Indian your name would have been Chief Peacemaker." He quickly replied and said, "And you would have been Squaw Stir'em Up." So we laugh now and say that those are our Indian names. He wanted to calm down his Squaw Stir'em Up, and I wanted to get Chief Peacemaker ready for a little war.

The Fear of the Lord

When we got down to truth, Rodney really wanted me to get free of my anger issues and I wanted him to get rid of passivity and appeasement. We also say that is when the fear of the Lord entered into our marriage. We began to see the deposit of God in each other. Rodney has a major deposit of Prince of Peace in him and I have a deposit of the Man of War in me. Both of our characteristics were deposits of Jesus. They needed healing and sanctification, but we began to honor them in each other and it began to make a huge difference.

It caused us to look at some other elements that are opposing qualities in Jesus:

Rodney	**Kathy**
Prince of Peace	Man of War
Mercy	Judgment
Wisdom	Revelation

Works	Faith
Kingship	Servanthood

These are very opposite qualities, but Jesus embodied them all. We often see these differences in marriages, especially those called to ministry. Without revelation and understanding, we can question those deposits of Jesus in our spouse. Can you imagine mercy and judgment parenting together, especially in a blended family? That was us. Thank God it didn't take us too long until we realized we had to pray a lot to find agreement. I remember early on feeling like Rodney would rain on my revelation parade. I would get all excited about something and it would feel so "now" because revelation always does and he would start talking about timing and process and it would feel like he just wasn't getting it. Now I know revelation without wisdom gets into trouble and wisdom with no revelation has nowhere to go. I would question Rodney's lack of faith at times because he would directly go to how it would get done. And then he would really confuse me because he operates in the gift of faith and at times had tremendous faith. I kept looking for the switch to that gift but it is clearly a manifestation of the spirit that I have no control over. But the Bible says that faith without works is dead.

As we began to honor each other related to spiritual gifting and the deposits of Jesus that we both had very naturally, the beautiful stuff began to happen and we began to become one. So now I'm more peaceful than ever before, and Rodney can confront issues in a way that he wasn't able to before. I walk in more wisdom and he walks in more revelation. I could go on and on but most importantly, we want you to stop and look at the deposits of God in each other. Where are you different? Where do you need healing so your deposit can shine?

Using the Tools

We encourage couples to use the DISC Personality Profile to determine and understand basic personality differences. It will give you a great basic understanding of your personality differences. It's another area where we are totally different. I am a high D and Rodney is an SIC. They are very different personality types. For example, D personalities love change and the S loves stability and can resist change. So in our world, some things stay the same, and other things change. I don't move Rodney's recliner unless there has been discussion and it's become really necessary, but the color of the wall behind it may change along with other things around it. D types are task oriented and like to multi-task and the S and I types are relationship orientated, which means for my husband to feel loved, I have to put down my iPhone at lunch or on a night out and give him some undivided attention. But then he often helps me figure out how I can get several things done at once and he has a happy woman who just got to multi-task. You don't learn about yourself or your spouse so you can always have it your way. You learn what areas require sacrifice and self-discipline. It doesn't give you the right to just say, "Well, that's just the way I am." We all have to be transformed into the image of Jesus Christ. It just helps us to know what areas we need to be transformed.

Once there's an understanding of what your personalities look like, we encourage you to go to LifeLanguages.com, which is an in-depth communication analysis, and complete their online profile. A good analogy between the two is discovering through the DISC Profile that you are ice cream, and then learning if you are chocolate, vanilla, chocolate chip mint, rocky road, etc. with Life Languages. After you have both taken the Life Languages profiles, you are able to submit both results for something called Cross Talk. It helps you see where communication is easy for you as a couple and also where you may have difficulty communicating.

The DISC Profile and Life Languages have both been life savers for our marriage, family, and for team building in ministry and business. Rather than spending more time discussing them in further detail, we encourage you to go to the websites at the end of this chapter and get further information yourself. At those sites, you will find profiles than you can take along with information to help you understand the results.

There's also the differences that we might have in our love languages. We like to use Gary Chapman's five different love languages. He's got a great website at 5lovelanguages.com. The five basic love languages are words of affirmation, quality time, receiving gifts, acts of service, and physical touch. My love language is acts of service and Rodney's is quality time and words of affirmation. Again, very different, but when you understand them, you can begin to love your spouse in ways that really touch their hearts. So many times, we try to love people the way we want to be loved. We give gifts because we want gifts. We praise because we want affirmation, but in a relationship, it's critical that we give our spouse what "they need and want." You can also take a quick profile on the 5 different languages of apology on the

5lovelanguages website which is also very interesting and helpful. It's amazing that we can even apologize differently. We've used the test in counseling and helped couples see that they are holding their spouse to their standard of what an apology looks like. The spouse may use a very different apology language and often feels like their apology is never received. This can cause big problems, but when there is understanding and communication, healing, restoration, and unity can flow.

By now you've probably noticed that we have not mentioned basic differences between men and women. There are two reasons for that. First, there is so much information on it you've probably already heard a bunch, and it's easily available online. Second, some of those differences have changed as culture has changed and sometimes it's more about the stereotypes than actual differences. Often some of those differences are really personality differences. For example, usually they say women are security oriented, but I'm a high D and I like adventure, change, and can live on the edge. We've minister to a number of couples where the man communicated much more out of his emotions and the woman communicated more out of logic. So yes, there are differences between men and women, but rather than just re-trumpet them, we are more interested in you diving into self-discovery and learning more about your mate's special flavor.

We have found that the more we are able to understand ourselves and then our differences, the more amazing our partnership has become. The tools listed below are also so helpful in parenting and working on a team, whether it's in business or ministry. It's given us so much more understanding of how to communicate and work with people in general. The beauty is that everything God has ever made is unique, one-of-a-kind; every flower, snowflake, mountain, and person. When we begin to celebrate our diversity and realize that unity isn't everyone becoming the same (which is conformity), but each part working together, we begin to receive the blessings of God that's spoken of in Psalm 133. In that chapter it says that God commands a blessing where there is unity. A marriage where He commands a blessing is much better than a marriage full of strife. And then we can change the title of this chapter to *"Thank God for Your Differences Because They Are Blessing Me."*

Go to DISCvaluesprofiles.com, LifeLanguages.com and 5Loveanguages.com for more information.

Ask Yourself

1. What differences between my spouse and I create the most problems?
2. How have I dishonored and disrespected those differences?
3. How can I begin to honor and respect those differences?
4. Do I have trouble accepting apologies from my spouse or problems believing that they are genuinely sorry?
5. Is our marriage important enough to invest some time in self-discovery by taking profiles that help me better understand myself and my spouse?

RODNEY & KATHY TOLLESON

CHAPTER SEVEN:
IDENTIFYING, UNDERSTANDING, AND MINISTERING TO TRIGGERS

We have a saying in the counseling room, "The 'it' is never the 'it'." What do we mean by that? It's simply that usually the presenting problem is never the real problem. It's simply fruit when there is usually much deeper root. Here are a couple of examples:

Example #1: A wife is controlling related to money. Normal counsel is to help create a budget and empower the husband regarding expenditures. But if the "it" is that she was raised in poverty and is operating in the shame-fear-control cycle, then all the budgets in the world wouldn't work. That root of shame and fear of poverty has to be exposed and ministered to for real partnership in the area of finances.

Example #2: A husband gets explosive whenever his wife adds or adjusts anything he says. You could counsel a wife to just not give any input in the relationship and try to adjust some of the fruit, but the real root is his older brother always over-powered him, talked over him, and he's never really dealt with it.

Example #3: A wife only wants affection from her husband, but withdraws from sexual advances. You could give Biblical counsel that it's important for them to have a sexual relationship in order to protect each other from sin and that a husband owns his wife's body. That's dealing with surface fruit if the root lies in past sexual abuse. And if the husband takes true spiritual responsibility and ownership for his wife's body, he will realize that it has been damaged and traumatized and it will take healing and understanding for her body to get well along with her mind and emotions. If he really loves his wife and cares about her body, he will help her seek healing and freedom.

Example #4: A husband gets crazy jealous over any attention his wife receives from another man. You can try to get her to curtail interactions with other men or to dress down, etc. You are simply trying to polish the fruit. When you get to the root, you might discover that his mother was unfaithful to his father and he was often times confronted with the need to lie for her and interact with some of her lovers. That bitter root judgment is at work and his heart needs forgiveness and healing to be set free.

Example #5: A husband shuts down whenever there's a holiday. A wife can keep trying to find some way to engage him, or get angry at him for disengaging and be upset about the fruit. Or they can discover that because of his alcoholic family holidays were always a painful time that created shame and disappointment. It was easier to disconnect and not feel. Once the root is identified and ministered to, he is able to engage and feel a part.

We could go on with examples in our own life and the lives of others related to the "it" not really being the "it." What we learned is that our over-reactions and under-reactions were signs that there was deeper wounding below the surface. The Bible says in Proverbs 27:6 that the wounds of a friend are faithful. We always say that they are faithful in finding our deeper wounds. Childish emotions and behavior are also signs that wounding from our childhood may have been triggered.

Wounded reactions were another area where our personality differences surfaced. When I (Kathy) was triggered, I could get very angry and sometimes it became pure rage. Pretty typical response for a wounded Man of War. My over-reactions were so outrageous when we first got married, we called them my Vietnam flashbacks. It was important for Rodney to not personalize them and because he wasn't in the Vietnam War, that labeling helped him. And it helped me not to carry shame for some of my reactions as I began to realize the damaged root system I had that needed healing.

Rodney on the other hand would shut down and withdraw. His response to, "Is there anything wrong?" would sound like this, "No, I'm just tired," or "Just not feeling well." There was always an excuse for his behavior. Usually it was so buried, he really didn't even realize he was triggered. He was a wounded Chief Peacemaker who didn't dare make any waves. His triggered response was so subtle I would have to watch his pretty blue eyes because they would become a little gray when he was upset. Now he's much more in touch and able to communicate what's going on inside.

Emotional Accountability

In the beginning stages, I could easily blame my anger on others because, of course, if they hadn't done or said this or that, I wouldn't have gotten angry. Rodney simply buried his emotions and would just disconnect and act surprised if I thought anything might be amiss. But as we began to get more healing, we came to a place in our marriage that required a higher standard. After all, "I'm sorry" can wear off pretty quickly in a marriage, especially when there is no change.

We began to take ownership for our responses and the fruit of our own reactions and emotions. That required truth in our inward parts which the Bible talks about in Psalm 51:6. I had to own my anger and rage and not blame it on anyone else. Then when I over-reacted, I had to get with the Holy Spirit to help Him show me my wounded root system. What had happened in my life that caused me to over-react that way? And guess what - I found Him faithful! We've been married over thirty years and my first big over-reaction was about nine months into the marriage. (Thank God for honeymoon periods!) That's when we came up with my Vietnam flashbacks. God was faithful to show me what had happened in my past that caused me to over-react. We were at a seminar in Alabama at the time and I was so angry that I was ready to drive home to Florida, pack up my two daughters and leave the marriage. When the Lord showed me the past painful memory, it all made sense. I was ready to leave over something that was nothing, except it touched something that had been a lot, a lot of pain, a lot of repressed anger, and a lot of emotional abuse.

A Healing Journey

It was absolutely so amazing to me as I began my healing journey to discover that the Holy Spirit really did know every hair on my head and everything that had ever happened to me. The memories that I had long forgotten would be dropped into my Spirit every time I went in prayer to help figure out what had caused such ugly fruit. After the wounded place was identified, I would express my feelings to the Lord and forgive those involved. Then I could ask Jesus to bring the healing and He would always come and minister to me. Many times I would literally see Him in the memory. Years later, we met Chester and Betsy Kylstra. In their *Restoring the Foundations-Integrated Ministry Process*, they called that area of ministry, "soul/spirit hurts." We encourage you to go to their website at *RestoringtheFoundations.org* for more information.

Rodney always says that we concentrated on me for the first five years and he didn't think he had any problems, then the Lord came for him. He began the same process and had to take ownership when he disconnected, shut-down emotionally, or withdrew. He was an under-reactor which went perfectly with his personality. At first, it took him time to get in touch with the fact that something had triggered one of his inner hurts, but once he did and started asking the Lord to reveal what the real problem was, he was on a roll. Mr. Passivity turned into a true Prince of Peace and even wrote a book called, *"Passivity, A Silent Killer."* He was amazed at the supernatural recall he received related to his reactions. And together we have been on a shame free healing journey ever since. We've discovered that when you truly fall in love with your Healer, you're no longer concerned with how long the journey is, you just begin to enjoy it. Now if we are both triggered about something, we can actually say, "I think you're more triggered than I am, let's deal with yours and then come back and get my issue." Most major fights with couples are when they are both triggered and the minor ones are when one of them is triggered.

We have to get emotionally honest even when we can control the outside behavior or dialogue because sometimes it's just childish feelings and thoughts on the inside. We have to really get to the truth in the inward parts. I remember telling Rodney one night that he should be so glad I was a Christian so the whole neighborhood wouldn't hear everything I was calling him in my head at that moment. I couldn't just pretend it wasn't happening because it wouldn't lead to more healing. I had gotten hooked on healing and wasn't going to let pride or shame stop me from confessing what was going on even if he couldn't hear it. And from that place of emotional honesty, the Lord showed me where the real issue was; a real ugly, damaged root from childhood that created the name calling in my head. It didn't really have anything to do with him – it was all a reaction to stuff that had happened in the past. We can live in denial. We can blame shift. We can project. We can spin all of our behavior with justification or we can create our own no-spin zone and become emotionally honest and accountable; it's mandatory operating procedure for a healing journey. Sometimes we wonder and whine that God isn't really healing us, but He can't in an atmosphere of secrecy, lies, manipulation, and hiding behind our pathetic fig leaves.

Stumbling Blocks

The stumbling blocks to healing happen when we justify or deny our responses or when we blame our reactions on others. We have to learn to own it all. We also can't just identify the real root issue; we have to make sure we allow Jesus to minister to us. That takes the prophetic anointing because we need to be able to hear Him, see Him, feel Him, or all of the above. He alone is our Healer. We can't heal ourselves and we surely can't heal each other. In the earlier years, sometimes I was so triggered I had to get alone with the Lord to process what really caused it and to work through to healing, or maybe talk it out with another safe person. Most of the time now, we can share in each other's healing process but are both also able to receive ministry alone with the Lord.

Another stumbling block to healing is using addictive behavior to mask our pain. As Christians, maybe we've gotten past the alcohol or drug use, but now we are eating, working on a computer, watching TV, or doing something to escape. We have to recognize and call ourselves and our spouse out when we realize we are trying to escape. All of those things are fine at the right time and the right proportion, but not when they are used so we don't have to deal with our issues.

Authentic Selves = Authentic Marriage

The more we receive healing the more authentic we can be as individuals. It also allows us to be more productive and also balances our life with greater rest. When we don't have to try to cover for our own or our spouse's woundedness, we no longer have to walk on egg shells. The more healing I received, the easier it was for me to be the true Man of War that God had created me to be without taking my warfare out on everybody else. I was then able to become much more effective as a spiritual warrior and a lot safer for my family and others. The more healing Rodney received, the easier it was him for to be that Prince of Peace without appeasement and passivity. He was able to walk in his leadership anointing with a lot more ease and grace. In his book on passivity, he shared that he had been the Rolaid King. On the outside he could keep smiling, but on the inside, he always had internal stress. Thank God that's a thing of the past. The Lord has been so good to two broken people. I (Kathy) had gotten pregnant at seventeen and was in a very immature, volatile marriage that included alcohol. After I was divorced, I became a Christian. Rodney had two marriages and three sons by the time he was twenty-three and had become a backslidden Baptist. We understand brokenness; we understand blended families; we understand past triggers; we understand differences in personality; we understand the pressures of business and of ministry; we understand cultural differences- (I was raised in Northern Minnesota and Rodney was raised in Alabama – need I say more.); we understand that marriage isn't easy; but most of all we have come to understand with God all things are possible. HALLELUJAH!

You may need further ministry and equipping in this area and for further resources please go to *RestoringtheFoundations.org*.

Ask Yourself

1. How do I respond to triggers? Am I outwardly upset or do I keep everything inside?
2. What would scare me about being emotionally accountable?
3. What are the things in my childhood that I may need healing from?
4. What are the areas from past relationships that may be still affecting me?
5. Who would I look like if I was my healed authentic self?

CHAPTER EIGHT: UNPACK IT

We have to unpack our past. We wish you could leave it outside the door of your marriage, but it just doesn't work that way. Besides discovering emotional and mental wounding there are two other major areas that are important for us to unpack. The first we're going to share about relates to generational sin, how it affects us, and what we need to do to access freedom. The second is our belief systems that develop as a result of our childhood experiences and how they can still contaminate us and our relationships today. In case you haven't noticed, the wonderful thing about working on yourself in order to help your marriage relationship is that it helps you in every other area of your life, too. Marriage work may not always be easy, but it comes with a great benefit package.

Generational Iniquity

When we marry, two different generational lines come together, and with that, issues can be compounded. What if on one side there had never been a divorce and on the other side there were multiple divorces? What if on both sides there was anger, abuse, and control? What if one side had very occult practices and the other side was extremely religious? What if one side came from a stoic ancestry and the other was full of sexual sin? You get the picture. That's some baggage you want to unpack, not just from the emotional perspective we talked about related to triggers, but from the spiritual perspective. Sin is a specific act; iniquity is sinful patterns of behavior. Generational iniquity opens the door to generational curses.

Here are a few scriptures related to generational iniquity:

Leviticus 26:39-42 *And those of you who are left shall waste away in their iniquity in your enemies' lands; also in their fathers' iniquities, what* are with them, they shall waste away. 'But if they confess their iniquity and the iniquity of their fathers, with their unfaithfulness in which they were unfaithful to Me, and they also have walked contrary to them and have brought them into the land of their enemies; if their uncircumcised hearts are humbled, and they accept their guilt- then I will remember My covenant with Jacob, and My covenant with Isaac and My covenant with Abraham I will remember; I will remember the land.

Exodus 20:5-6 *you shall not bow down to them nor serve them. For I, the LORD your God, am a jealous God, visiting the iniquity of the fathers upon the children to the third and fourth generations of those who hate Me, but showing mercy to thousands, to those who love Me and keep My commandments.*

Lamentations 5:7 *Our fathers have sinned, and are no more; But we bear their iniquities."*

Jeremiah 14:20 *We acknowledge, O LORD, our wickedness and the iniquity of our fathers, for we have sinned against You.*

We could go on and on with scriptures related to generational iniquity, but we need to know the Good News. It's one of the reasons we should be so in love with Jesus, because on the Cross He bought redemption for us.

Galatians 3:13-14 *Christ has redeemed us from the curse of the law, having become a curse for us (for it is written, "Cursed is everyone who hangs on a tree), that the blessing of Abraham might come upon the Gentiles in Christ Jesus, that we might receive the promise of the Spirit through faith.*

Isaiah 61:4 *And they shall rebuild the old ruins, They shall raise up the former desolations, And they shall repair the ruined cities, The desolations of many generations.*

Ezekiel 18:29-30 *Repent, and turn yourselves from all your transgressions; so iniquity shall not be your ruin.*

Praise the Lord, Jesus is the antidote. But we have to understand everything He did on the Cross has to be appropriated. Everyone is not saved because Jesus died on the cross. It takes personal appropriation by faith. People often tell us, "Well that's all under the blood," (even though the fruit of their lives demonstrates the contrary), and we like to ask, "When did you put it there?" You may have sang "Redeemed, I'm Redeemed" in church, but if you haven't appropriated the blood through repentance, that curse still has power over you and your generations. If you have ever felt like you're cursed in an area – you probably are. Take the time to examine generational patterns of iniquity, and take that sin to the Cross through repentance. Forgive your ancestors for all the pain and issues that resulted from their iniquity, ask forgiveness for any involvement you previously had related to the iniquitous pattern and open your heart to the generational blessings He has for you.

In my own life (Kathy), one of the generational patterns of iniquity was illegitimacy which has powerful repercussions. In Deuteronomy 23:2, the Bible tells us that one of illegitimate birth cannot enter into the assembly of the Lord even to the tenth generation. That's eight hundred and twenty-eight people. That might mean there's a good chance of some illegitimacy in your family lineage. Ever have trouble feeling a part of church life? Ever have trouble entering into the presence of the Lord during worship? It wouldn't hurt to repent of any generational illegitimacy because it gives the enemy legal ground to harass you in this area.

We had pastored for four years before our oldest daughter, Leanne, ever darkened the door of our church. Once I repented for the iniquity pattern of illegitimacy, she was back home, in church, and hasn't left the House of the Lord since. That's powerful.

We have seen over and over again how repenting of generational iniquity released freedom to couples and their families in so very many areas. It's not necessary to labor under the curse when all we have to do is repent and ask Jesus to forgive the iniquity. The Bible talks about the heavy weight of sin and often because of lack of knowledge we still carry the baggage of generational iniquity. It's time to unpack those bags. You may be saying, "I don't really know a lot about my ancestors." It doesn't matter, the Holy Spirit does and He can show you what you might be missing. And one of the best ways is to look at the iniquitous patterns that you are fighting right now. What's happening in your children's lives, maybe even your grandchildren's? We have yet to minister to anyone that had a sin issue that they just couldn't get free of that didn't have generational iniquity. Once it's taken to the Cross through repentance they discover the truth of the Scripture that tells us His yoke is easy and His burden is light, Matthew 11:30. What are you waiting for? Start unpacking!

Our Belief System

All the experiences we have as children create belief systems about a lot of stuff. Through our experiences we develop a whole world view: who we are, what God is like, who men are like, who women are like, who we can trust and who we can't. If we grew up in poverty, we might believe there's not enough to go around; someone's always left out. If we were raised with a father who was dominant and always in control, we might have the belief that men are controlling and you always have to be subservient to them. If your mother was abusive, your heart may have learned that you can't really trust women because they will always hurt you.

In secular counseling, these things may be called irrational beliefs or unhealthy cognitions (thoughts). I like what Chester and Betsy Kylstra call them in *Restoring the Foundations Ministry*. They call them ungodly beliefs. Once they are identified, then the Lord can speak truth to our hearts and we can receive new Godly beliefs. Thank God, He has given us minds that can be renewed and hearts that can receive revelation.

When we are children, we learn more with our hearts than our heads. That's why it's so hard to deal with deep messages from childhood. It's one of the reasons we all love revelation. Revelation is when our heart learns something new. It's more than just information to file away in our head. If we've heard that we are stupid all of our lives, it will take revelation from the Lord that He created us in His image with amazing intelligence.

We went through the *Restoring the Foundations Integrated Ministry* over twenty years ago and you will still find on Rodney's desk and my dresser some more new Godly beliefs that we are working on today. It's not a one-time fix because we are all riddled with so many ungodly beliefs. We minister *Restoring the Foundations* to couples and find amazing things happen when we uncover their ungodly belief systems and help them receive new Godly ones.

Here's one of my (Kathy) basic ones, "I am the problem." Can you imagine having a discussion with someone who is already defensive because they are ready to hear that they are the problem? It was also a good reason not to get involved in some things because who wants to end up the problem. Did I know it was there? No, but it was still controlling things. Because the Holy Spirit is faithful, He revealed it. I have a simple new Godly belief, "I am a blessing." I kept confessing it, believing it, reading it, and now I know that's true. That's who the Lord originally created me to be.

One of Rodney's major ungoldy beliefs was, "Nothing good every comes out of confrontation." Well, from what we've previously shared, I'm sure you can see how well that one worked out for us. He wanted to avoid everything and I wanted to confront everything. His new Godly belief is, "There is Godly fruit in Godly confrontation." It was life-changing for him and marriage changing for us.

When we have beliefs that do not align with the Word and with the Lord's nature and character, we are going to have problems in life. We may not always be consciously aware of them, but they are lurking just below the surface causing us to have ungodly expectations in areas that can affect our behavior and the behavior of others. If you're married to someone who has been rejected most of their life, they probably have the ungodly belief that everyone will reject them eventually. You know what it's like to feel that bitter root trying to defile you and cause you to reject when it's not even in your heart. Hebrews 12:15 *looking carefully lest anyone fall short of the grace of God; lest any root of bitterness springing up cause trouble, and by this many become defiled;*

If you're going to renew or restore a marriage, it's going to take renewing of the mind. You can't expect change without creating change. The old you needs to become the new you. Remember, marriage is you and you together. Change you and the marriage is changed. Both of you make changes and you have exponential change.

It's so empowering when you know you can change your world by changing your mind. It's almost so easy people bypass it because it couldn't be that simple, but it is. We were created in the image and likeness of God, Himself. Our thoughts and confession have the ability to create the world we live in and if we don't like that world, we have the power to change it. Whenever we can help couples change their belief systems, we see major changes in the marriage.

If one side of the suitcase is generational iniquity, and the other side is our stinkin' thinking, when we unpack them both we are on the road to a much easier life and marriage. Stop fighting, surrender to the process of God. It's so much easier just to deal with your stuff. When peace, joy, and righteousness, which make up the Kingdom of God, are more important than family pride, being right, stubbornness, etc., you are on your way to a Kingdom Marriage!

1. What are areas of generational iniquity in my family line and have I taken them to the Cross through repentance?
2. Am I still dealing with shame related to issues in my family?
3. Could I have any ungodly beliefs related to marriage from my childhood?
4. Could I have any ungodly beliefs about men or women related to my childhood?
5. What areas am I having problems in now that could be a result of ungodly beliefs?

CHAPTER NINE:
LEFTOVERS

Some dishes taste great as leftovers but serving up leftovers in a marriage doesn't work. One of the marriage problems we find over and over and again is that couples allow everything else in their life to take precedent. The marriage gets the leftovers in time, resources, finances and attention. It takes two very important elements to have a healthy marriage and that's priorities and boundaries.

Priorities Make the Difference

In a healthy spiritual marriage, the marriage relationship is placed second under their individual relationship with the Lord. The relationship with their immediate family is next and other relationships like extended family, spiritual relationships, friendships, business and ministry relationships follow. It makes common sense. Without a relationship with the Lord, it's impossible to really "do" marriage. Marriage was ordained by God. It's governed by Him. And it takes a supernatural act of becoming one with another human being. Wow – try that without Him! That's exactly what most people do and then wonder why they have such problems. They meet with Him at the altar for the wedding and then say, "See ya," and head off for a marriage relationship that either doesn't involve Him at all or only does so minimally. Most marriages do not end up in two human beings becoming one, but ends up in divorce: two individuals living in marital hell, two individuals who have become business or ministry partners, two roommates, two people raising children together, etc. – but not marriage as God designed it. So putting God first is essential for moving on to the next relationship.

The next building block is the marriage relationship, without it being a priority there are problems in the family relationships. If the marriage isn't solid, the family isn't solid. So after our relationship with the Lord, our relationship with our spouse should take the next highest priority. In business, when something is a priority, it gets personnel, resources, time, and money. If you're in a marriage and you never allocate time, money, and resources for it, your marriage is not a priority. And if you make your children the excuse, you are not giving them the most important element which is their father and mother in a strong personal relationship. My great grandmother always said that the best thing a father can do for his children is to love their mother and vice versa. Pretty sound advice. I hear excuses all the time. We just don't have time because of the kids. We never have extra money to spend on us. Those are choices, and many times they are easy walls to help avoid intimacy.

It's not about how much money you spend, it's the priority. If it's ten dollars for frozen yogurt on a Friday night for two hours together while someone babysits, and that's all you can afford, you still have created time for you and your spouse to be together. Sometimes money and resources might be strapped but creativity can then abound. A put the kids to bed early night, a $1.50 movie rental and a bag of popcorn can turn into a great night. Throw in a candle and take time to groom yourself and its date night. Most importantly, take time to pray together and talk together. A walk doesn't cost anything and it's a great time to talk. If there's a marriage dvd that might help, buy it and watch it. If there's a marriage retreat, sign-up, even if it's to make a good marriage better. INVEST in each other and your marriage.

We always encourage couples with children to create an atmosphere of healthy boundaries. Teach children never to enter your bedroom without knocking and asking permission to come in, and to not interrupt if you are communicating with each other. Also, put your young children to bed early enough to have a couple of hours alone before bedtime. If you go to bed the same time your children do, you will rob yourself of important Daddy and Mommy time. As your children get older, have a certain time when it's time to go to your room. They might stay up later, but it gives you as a couple a time for some privacy. Kids will not establish boundaries. It's your job to establish and enforce them.

From the marriage relationship you can then establish your immediate family as your next priority. Not every marriage produces children, but the majority do. They should come next - not the ministry, not your job, not your business, but your family. We always say that one day you will pay the piper. You will either spend time with your children as part of your daily life or you will spend time with them in a counseling room, a juvenile detention center, or a visitation center at a jail or prison. Or you will have the painful outcome of reaping what you sowed and you will not be a priority in their life. They will not have time for you as they grow-up. After the family, then we can allocate for the rest of the world.

This may not always look like equal time segments: two hours for you, and two hours for you, and two hours for that. But it is knowing what is important. I have confidence as Rodney's wife that after the Lord, I am his next priority which actually gives me the freedom to release him to other relationships and activities. He knows that after the Lord, I have him as my next priority and as a result, he releases me to tremendous freedom when it comes to extended family and ministry. When we create healthy priorities, it drives out jealousy, manipulation, control, and competition. I don't have to compete with other relationships and he doesn't have to be jealous of my times related to ministry. We can be secure with each other because we have made our relationship a priority with more than just words. It didn't happen overnight; it takes a series of intentional choices to solidify relationship priorities.

Setting and Enforcing Boundaries

If you don't set boundaries in your life, leftovers will be all you can serve each other. No one else will set your boundaries for your marriage. Your kids won't say, "Dad and Mom, you really need a night out together." They will probably be crying as you walk out the door. Your boss won't say, "Hey, don't work so much overtime, it's probably not healthy for your marriage." And unless it's a real healthy church, most of the time you won't hear, "Hey, we can get this done without you, go home and spend some time together." There's demands are everywhere and it's up to us to establish boundaries so that we have enough time and energy for our marriage relationship. Sometimes you have to ask yourself, "Looking at how I set boundaries and prioritize, is my marriage really the most important relationship after God?"

In our digital age, sometimes we have to take authority over our electronic devices or we never have a conversation that's not interrupted by a text, a phone call, or something new being downloaded. There's a time to leave the electronics in another room or go to dinner and leave them in the car. We know right now you're saying, "But we have small children and there might be an emergency."

Solution: Have the least digitally addicted spouse keep their phone on them, keep the ringer off, and look at it every ten minutes. Don't respond to anything else, just check if there's an emergency text. If you want uninterrupted time, you can find it. I will repeat, children and other interruptions are a great way to avoid intimacy when the marriage is starting to fray.

People often see boundaries as rejection or not being loving. It's the total contrary. When healthy boundaries are set and enforced, there is no need to create walls, and relationships remain healthy over the long run. Divorce is really a relationship wall and usually you will find a trail of broken boundaries on the other side of it. Parents who don't set boundaries with their children create a stressful environment for the whole family where crisis, chaos, and strife abound.

Boundaries can be related to how we speak to one another, how we treat each other physically, time and space, privacy, the ability to have rights that aren't violated, etc. If parents require their children to spend some time in their rooms so that they can have an adult conversation, that's not rejection, that's healthy parenting. If not, the parents are sharing some real heavy duty stuff that the child might not be able to handle emotional or process mentally. You might have had a family disagreement and then get over it, but the child is now uncomfortable around his aunt or uncle. We know from personal experience that it was pretty apparent when children had been privy to adult conversations related to the church or us as their pastors by the way the children began to change in their response to us. It was very sad because it robbed the children of innocence they should have been able to keep. Boundaries help keep everyone safe. You can't really do marriage or family without them.

Investment

It's apparent that in many marriages, the biggest investment of time, energy, and money came before and during the wedding, and then everyone starts making withdrawals. A husband used to romance his wife and now he just wants to come home, eat dinner, not help around the house, and demand sex because she's his wife and that's her duty. A wife doted on every word her husband said, dressed up, fixed up, and gave him top priority, now she barely grooms herself and can barely look up from her I-Phone. And we wonder why our marriage isn't working. It's because we stopped working; we stopped investing. A great marriage takes a great investment, it's as simple as that.

Hebraic culture had it right. In the first year of marriage, the groom did not work. During the betrothal period he would go and prepare a place for his bride. Usually it was adding a room onto his father's house, but once that year was over the wedding took place. The next year was spent on his bride. She was his focus which, if he used the time wisely, would make for one very secure wife. A day is like a thousand years to the Lord, the Millennial Reign will be a thousand years and our Bridegroom, Jesus Christ, will have His total focus on us, His Bride. (Revelation 20:4)

Priorities are so important. If our marriage is not a priority, we won't invest in it. If savings aren't a priority, we won't save. If our home isn't a priority, we won't invest in it, and this is one area many men don't have a revelation of that's critical for a good marriage. To a woman the home is an extension of her – it is the nest and she wants a man who cares about the nest. Many men neglect the nest or resist investment in it. That's not a smart man. We always encourage men who hire someone to take care of things around the house to still take some time to be personally involved. Whether it's in the planning or some actual doing, it's important. It doesn't take a lot of energy to look at some paint swatches, but to the woman you are showing interest in the nest. If it's an extension of her, you are showing interest in her. Have you ever asked yourself how the pool guy, the contractor, or the plumber, became so attractive to some woman that she had an affair with him? That's an easy answer; they were investing energy into the nest and they were caring for the nest. We don't care how much money you make, it's sexy to a woman when you do something around the house or yard that demonstrates that the nest is important to you.

It would be great if the recommendation was that whatever was spent on a wedding and a honeymoon had to be matched with at least half that amount to spend on the marriage in the first year. That could make a major difference. People often spend so much money and create debt for an extravagant wedding that they end up in financial stress the first year of marriage. A wedding is an event, but a marriage is for a lifetime.

In conclusion, if you don't want a marriage that is just the leftovers of life, it's essential to have your relationship as a top priority; first the Lord and then your spouse. It's also important to set and enforce healthy boundaries in order to not allow your marriage and family to be over-run by in-laws, friends, obligations, hobbies, and anything else that might infringe upon it. And then finally, what are you willing to invest? How important is your marriage? What value do you place on it? You can't expect to just withdraw and withdraw without one day finding yourself filing marital bankruptcy.

1. Is our first priority after our relationship with the Lord, our marriage?
2. How and when do we invest in our marriage relationship?
3. How would we rate ourselves in setting boundaries with our children, family, friends, and other relationships when it comes to our marriage?
4. How do we rate ourselves related to marriage investment? How does that rate compare to investment prior to the wedding?
5. What small incremental steps could we take related to marriage investment?

CHAPTER TEN:
SEX: Unafraid & Unashamed

We have found that physical intimacy needs a good foundation of spiritual, emotional, and mental intimacy for it to be truly what the Lord intended. Yes, it's true that when husbands and wives pray together, worship together, really talk about issues and allow healing and restoration in their lives, their sex lives improve. The more intimate they are in other areas automatically spills over into the sexual arena. A lot of couples want to fix sexual issues without dealing with the lack of intimacy in so many other areas of their lives. Sorry, it wasn't designed to work that way. We were created for covenant sexuality. A man and woman committed to being faithful to each other all the days of their lives.

Understanding Imprinting

Because we were created for covenant sexuality, we were designed with a sexual imprinting mechanism. This means that our first time sexual contact or sexual imprinting creates a desire in us to go back to that original imprinting. That's why pre-marital sex, masturbation, pornography and other sexual sins can be so destructive. The imprinting creates an extremely strong desire to go back to what created the original arousal.

Just imagine God creating man and woman and saying, "Now be in covenant with each other and be faithful to each other, but I'm going to make it hard as hell." That doesn't sound like a good, loving God. No, He made us so that it wouldn't be difficult if our first sexual exposure was with our covenant spouse. We know that's almost hard to imagine in our over-sexualized society. But He wouldn't have given us all the instruction and commands related to sex, purity, and holiness if it wasn't for a purpose. He knew how He created us.

Aren't you glad, you serve a God that can make all things new? Aren't you excited that nothing is impossible with Him? Aren't you blessed today that He is a God of restoration. If you know that your sexuality was imprinted out of the will of God, you can repent of any sexual sin, forgive anyone who could have sexually damaged you, and ask the Lord to wipe your sexual slate clean. If you and your spouse have faith, pray over each other. Ask the Lord to send the fire of God to cleanse and renew. Let His power touch you- spirit, soul, and body. You can lay hands on your spouse and insert their name or insert your name in the following prayer. It is a sample I use in my book, *Restoring Sexuality*:

Lord, I bring (name) sexuality before your throne. I ask you to wipe the slate clean. Send your fire to purify all of (his/her) desires. Touch (his/her) mind, memories, emotions, and (his/her) body and spirit and make it clean. I thank you Lord that you make all things new. I ask you to make (name)'s sexuality brand new. I pray that the next time we come together covenant sexuality will be written on our spirit, soul, and body. I ask you to restore (his/her) passion and to give (him/her) freedom to express (himself/herself) sexually. We thank you for a new beginning, Lord.

Anointed Sex

Sometimes people have trouble with the use of those two words in the same sentence. But in a Kingdom Marriage we should expect anointed sex. The anointing makes everything better: worship, preaching, fellowship, etc. God designed us with sex in mind and when we get a revelation that our sexual union is as much a spiritual activity as it is physical, our sex life will improve dramatically. Here are some thoughts to help you. First, pray over your marriage bed, anoint it with oil, dedicate it to the Lord. Play anointed instrumental worship music and create a spiritual atmosphere. It's okay to be sexy, but it doesn't have to be lustful. There's a difference. We can have respect, love, and healthy boundaries and still have a great sex life. We know too many Christians who still use pornography or alcohol to try to enhance their sex lives. It never does in the long-run. Only true intimacy brings the deep down satisfaction that our spirit and soul long for, and it's something that sexual acrobatics or fantasy can never deliver.

What about your bedroom? Can you walk in the room and sense the presence of God? Our kids call our bedroom the Holy of Holies. Our downstairs area was the Outer Court and the upstairs family area was deemed Inner Court. That means our bedroom wasn't a high traffic area, you could sense the Lord's presence, you treated the area respectfully, and it was a special place.

We always encourage couples to get the television out of the bedroom, get the office out of the bedroom, get your children out of your bed, and create a special intimate place where both the husband and wife feel comfortable. If it's over frilly, the woman may love it, but the husband might feel like an intruder. The physical bedroom is often a reflection of the sexual relationship between a man and a woman. We've been in beautifully decorated homes and find a bedroom with a sheet tacked up for drapes, and stuff piled all over because they hadn't gotten to it yet. And we are not talking that they had just recently moved into the home. It was just not a high value area. We call it the barren bedroom syndrome.

If you value your marriage and it is a priority, then your bedroom should be a priority. When is the last time it had a fresh coat of paint, a new bed covering, a new mattress? Is it a place where the two of you can pray together, have quiet time together, and enjoy your physical intimacy together? If not, make an investment in your bedroom because it is representative of your intimacy. It shouldn't just be a place you sleep at night, and it shouldn't be a place where you try to avoid each other. Make sure there's a lock on the door, children are taught to knock, and everyone in the house knows that they only enter with permission. Your bedroom should not be a thoroughfare. Even if you are sleeping in a one room house, you can find something to hang to create privacy and you can find something that looks good as easily as something ugly. Where ever you are and in whatever condition you find yourself in, there are ways to create privacy and beauty if it's truly a priority.

The Benefits

Often we hear couples complain that they are too tired or too busy for sex. And many of them are very young. Our motto is that if we are too busy or too tired for sex than we are too busy and our schedule needs adjusting. Sure, there are sometimes we are all busier than others. We may be affected by health issues or travel schedules, but we are talking about the norm not the occasional situation.

We also have a responsibility to stay healthy enough to participate in our sexual relationship. Watching our nutrition and making sure we have enough exercise is all a part of it. At the writing of this book, Rodney is sixty-eight and I'm sixty-three, and our sex life has improved as our relationship and health has improved. It can get better and better. But we have to live intentionally and make right choices which is why establishing priorities is so important.

Our God created us with amazing detail. Everything works together for our good. It's so apparent related to our sexuality. Our brain is wired so that touch and orgasm create chemical releases that are critical to the relationship. Three of the main ones are dopamine, serotonin and oxytocin:

Dopamine is released at the time of orgasm. It's the Woohoo!, I feel good chemical. It lights up the same reward center in the brain as heroin or cocaine. Yes, that's why sexual activity can be addictive and balance and wisdom is important.

Serotonin helps create a sense of calm and over-all well-being. It wards off depression. You could say more satisfying sex leads to less Prozac.

Oxytocin is also released through touch, genital stimulation, and orgasm. It has been called "the cuddle hormone" and it helps with bonding, trust, and relaxation. It counteracts cortisol or the stress hormone. It's the same hormone that is released in a mother and an infant when the child is nursed.

So God created our human bodies to release a hormone that creates trust and bonding with our spouse when we have sex. Our spouse activates the reward centers of our brain during sexual intimacy causing us to be attracted to them, and then our relationship helps us to have an over-all sense of well-being. I would say that's a great deal of benefit.

The other benefit is not physical, it is spiritual. Our sexual union is a prophetic demonstration of two becoming one. As we join together sexually there is a transference of spirit. That is why it is so important to be careful related to who you have sex with because you begin to become like them. You carry a piece of them with you. That's why it's important to break sexual ties with anyone you have previously been sexually intimate with prior to your marriage. Here's a quick sample prayer:

Sexual Tie Prayer

In the Name of Jesus, I confess all of my ungodly sexual ties. I ask you to forgive me and I forgive all of those involved _____. I separate myself from them spirit, soul, and body. I break all ungodly sexual or soulish ties to any other items that were related to ungodly sexual activity. Lord, please cleanse me and help me forget any ungodly relationships. I renounce any demonic entities that could have entered my life through sexual ties and command them to leave me now. Thank you Lord for your mercy and grace as you cleanse and restore me.

Damage and Abuse

You may have just skipped that last chapter or may have gotten angry while reading it. You might be thinking, "They just don't understand." Yes, we do! We have ministered to hundreds of people who have been abused, molested, or damaged in some way sexually. And we understand many people reading this book may be struggling in this area, but that doesn't change God's original plan and there is hope and healing in Him. We have seen first-hand, marriages where passion has been restored, walls became healthy boundaries, and addictions no longer ruled. There is freedom in Christ. We just have to get over our shame and let Him into those areas.

We need our trauma ministered to, and healing for our damage and brokenness. We need to replace ungodly beliefs with new Godly beliefs. Truth, not our childhood facts, has to reign in our lives. The fact might have been that as a child all anyone wanted from you was their own sexual gratification, but truth is that in your marriage you have so much more to offer. You are an amazing spiritual being created in the image of God. Fact might have been that masturbation helped you cope with a chaotic, stressful childhood, but truth is holiness and a healthy sexual life with your spouse creates peace and joy. It's time to renew your mind and unpack any baggage you may have in this area.

You may need some help. Find someone in your area who has a reputation for being able to minister to those with damage in this area. Don't neglect it. Don't avoid it. There is hope for the broken and God is well equipped to minister to you. There are many resources you can find online to begin your journey. It's never too late, we encourage you not to give up.

We have worked with people who have been severely abused and traumatized and yet have seen the power of God at work to heal, restore, and redeem. For further help and ministry related to sexual issues, you can order *Restoring Sexuality* by Kathleen Tolleson from KingdomLifeNow.com or Amazon.com.

Ask Yourself

1. **If I had to rate our sex life from 1-10 what number would I give it?**
2. **What would I need to bring that number up to a 9 or 10?**
3. **Are there any areas in which I haven't been honest with my spouse related to our sexual life?**
4. **What was my first sexual imprinting (not necessarily the first time I experienced the sexual act)? Pray and ask the Lord to help you.**
5. **What does our bedroom need to make it a more special, intimate place?**

CHAPTER ELEVEN:
CRACKS IN THE FOUNDATION

New research shows that Christians have about a 15-20% divorce rate. For secular marriages, that statistic is between 20-25%. It's actually been improving since the 70's and 80's. Before we get too happy though, we have to remember that more and more people are living together without marriage, which had a greater social stigma in times past. Why are we sharing this information? Because it's critical for the church to look at how we do marriage from beginning to end. If we do it like the world, we will get worldly results. If we want Kingdom marriages, we have to do it in a Kingdom way. Using a worldly system trying to get a Godly marriage is simply self-defeating.

Dating versus Courtship

Let's start at the very beginning with what often tends to be a very unpopular topic, dating versus courtship. As pastors and counselors, we have seen first-hand, over and over again, the differences between the two concepts and how they affect marriage. Let's look at some of the differences.

First of all, in dating there's the continued practice of commitment and break-up, which, if you look at it in the big picture, just teaches people how to get ready for divorce. People may have practiced breaking-up a dozen or more times before the real deal. Secondly, dating teaches intimacy with no commitment and is focused on personal pleasure and enjoyment. People date to have fun, enjoy each other's company, avoid loneliness, and because it's a cultural norm. So, if you don't date, there must be something wrong with you. Or, could it be if you don't date, there's something really right with you? We know it's hard, the peer pressure isn't easy, and our culture, including the majority of churches, encourage and support the practice of dating. It's amazing that often the people who most resist the idea of courtship are those that are older and may have already been in one or more marriages. Their thought processes look a little like this, "I'm old enough to do this on my own; I don't need anyone else involved in my personal relationships." You would think they would be the last people to resist the idea. But we have found it not to be the case, so our encouragement is that courtship is a process that works regardless of age.

If you're going to change a broken system, it's important to look at it from beginning to end. And it all starts with how relationships are put together to begin with, and that's why it's important to look at dating and courtship. With courtship, the Lord, the family, and the church are brought into the process and each of these elements are often important in helping support a marriage relationship.

We've counseled so many people whose marriage had curses spoken over it from the start. Either a pastor, parents, family, or friends declared that it was doomed from the start and would never work out. Sure, they only wanted to help, but it plants a seed of doubt, and whenever the marriage suffers turbulence the couple remembers what was said and fear and anxiety creeps into the conversation. Doubt is placed in the foundation of the marriage. That's how the enemy attacked Adam and Eve in the garden, "Has God said?"

That's when you hear things like, "My mother said that I should never have married you in the first place. Our pastor wouldn't even marry us, we are cursed.

Your family never accepted me, that's why I won't go to holiday gatherings. Even my best friend said this was never going to work." We could share a thousand variations of this theme because we've heard so many of them. It creates a fracture in the foundation. A proper courtship process avoids all of that.

First, courtship should not be entered into unless both parties really believe that this relationship is destined for marriage. Courtship would be entered into with family and pastoral support and agreement, giving the allowance that if something is uncovered during the courtship it is not a binding agreement. During courtship the couple, depending on family situations, would spend appropriate time with each other's family and friends, helping bring them on board. Church and ministry relationships should also be cultivated by attending each other's church when possible.

If all goes well with the courtship, it should lead to engagement. Then after a period of time, marriage preparation, wedding planning, and then the wedding ceremony. Notice that we put marriage preparation before wedding planning. Engaged couples often get so focused on each other and the wedding, they forget to take time to really prepare for the marriage. In our ministry, we always have put a high priority on marriage preparation and couples are always thankful afterwards.

Dating might look like dinner and a movie on Saturday night; everyone on their best behavior and smelling good. Courtship might look like serving on a mission trip together or spending time working on a family project. Dating puts on the best face; courtship focuses on exposing who we really are flaws and all. Dating is not a family or church event; courtship gets family, church, and friends involved. Daters like to be alone together; those in courtship use the protection of others to help keep the relationship pure. Dating creates rejection for one or both of the parties; courtship minimizes rejection because it ultimately is simply seeking the Lord's will. Dating creates robbery because if the relationship does not end up in marriage someone will have been robbed. Courtship protects yourself, the other party and your future spouses and should only be entered into with a spiritual witness and confirmation. We have ministered to so many people who wished they had never dated anyone else, lived with anyone else, and even they even wish they had never kissed anyone else. Golf takes practice, playing the piano takes practice, but marital intimacy should not be practiced with anyone but your spouse.

Violated Trust

Many people who have dated and had betrayals and breakups come into the marriage very damaged in their ability to trust. Even in a courtship relationship trust can be violated if both parties don't help protect each other's purity. Couples often begin to cross the line once they are engaged. The justification is that we are almost already married. We know this is where the relationship is heading and inappropriate physical intimacy starts happening. Sometimes it's because of pressure from one of the parties. Many times in sorting out marital issues, it's traced back to events that happened before the actual marriage. If you lay a foundation for a home and the concrete mix is not right and there's too much sand in the mix, or if there isn't enough re-bar laid in the concrete, the home that's built on it will eventually have problems. There will be cracks in the foundation which then creates shifting in the home, and cracks will begin to appear in ceilings and walls. The amount of problems in the house will depend on the condition of the foundation. We often see the same thing when it comes to marriages. There were problems in the foundation of the relationship.

It's Time to Take a Stand

In order for the culture to change in the Christian community, it's important that ministers begin to educate people on the differences between dating and courtship. The Bible gives no counsel to help people in relation to dating because it's not a Biblical principle. Self-gratification is not a Biblical standard and most reasons for dating go back to self. We have found that courtship is not a very popular stance, but once people really understand it, they get on board. We've seen some amazing results when people have walked through the courtship process and we have seen a couple of potential disasters averted. Sadly, we have ministered to many people whose hearts and lives have been torn up through the dating process. Soul ties have to be broken, forgiveness has to take place, often dating led to inappropriate physical intimacy that has to be dealt with, hearts have to be healed, and all of these things can be avoided if we adjust the process.

This chapter may have been too late for your process, but it can help you help others. You can help create a new cultural perspective with your children or people you may minister to, or influence. It can also help you find fractures in your own foundation and begin the repair process. Marriages are God's building block for families, for communities, and for the Kingdom. The relationship between Adam and Eve was established as the prototype for the human race. If we build our marriages on faulty foundations, everything we build on it will have problems.

It's like health prevention. We can eat a healthy diet and exercise and avoid diabetes or heart attacks or we can wait until we have health problems and then try to keep it under control with meds and/or surgery. We don't do the right stuff upfront and then it creates problems down the line. Let's get smart and let's help others do the right stuff and avoid the pitfalls. We can take a stand together.

Ask Yourself

1. What would some of the cracks in our marriage foundation be?
2. Is there anyone we need to forgive related to our marriage foundation?
3. In what areas was trust violated before our wedding? Repent and forgive.
4. Are there any word curses we have to break off of our marriage?
5. If dated prior to marriage is there any unfinished emotional business that needs to be taken care of? (Soul ties? Unforgiveness? Rejection? Broken heart issues? Guilt or Shame?)

CHAPTER TWELVE: MARRIAGE VISION

Vision is a critical element of any endeavor. Proverbs 29:18 tells us that people perish without a vision (KJ) and the NKJ says that people without a revelation cast off restraint. People in business are taught to have vision statements for their companies. Cities and towns bring in consultants and have visioning meetings to help get everyone moving in the same direction. Successful ministries have a vision that can be articulated by those involved. Habakkuk 2:2, "Then the Lord answered me and said: Write the vision and make it plain on tablets, that he may run who reads it."

God has given us His vision for marriage in Ephesians Chapter 5:31-32. Through the revelation of the Holy Spirit, the Apostle Paul shares that our earthly marriages are to be representative of the heavenly relationship between Jesus Christ and His Church. In scripture the church is often referred to as the Bride of Christ. It is a picture of a man laying down his life for his wife out of love, preferring her, offering her protection, provision, and care. In return she responds with a heart of respect and a desire to serve. And together they walk in God' original intention of dominion strengthened by their covenant with the Lord and each other.

So first we have to have revelation of God's vision for marriage, but just as we have to buy into the spreading of the Gospel as God's vision for the world, He still gives us an individual vision within His corporate vision and they will be in harmony. Just as a church or ministry has a corporate vision that embraces, supports, and serves many individual visions, our marriages work the same way.

All of us are called to accomplish different things. We have different gifts, passions, and purposes, just like ministries have different purposes and vision's within the Lord's vision for mankind. So our marriage may look different than someone else's.

Most of the time when couple's come for help their vision consists mainly of trying to survive the marriage relationship. They have no written or stated vision. They don't see their marriage as a vehicle the Lord wants to use in the earth to bring transformation to themselves and to fulfill a purpose. The biggest contribution their marriage brings to the Kingdom of God is to show up to church on a Sunday morning. They often fight before and after service, and it's not unusual for them to not be in agreement about where they are fellowshipping. They married to get their own personal needs fulfilled and then are angry and frustrated when the marriage relationship doesn't meet those needs.

When counseling, we always share that there are some things only God can do in our lives. We can co-labor with Him, but it just can't be done by human endeavor. You can't heal abandonment issues in your spouse – it takes God. You can't deliver your spouse from fear – it takes God. You can't bring conviction to your spouse to let go of unforgiveness and bitterness – it takes God. Marriage is designed to meet certain needs, but it has limitations and if you demand things from your spouse and marriage that only God can meet, you will live in continual disappointment and frustration.

One of the most important things you can do for your marriage is to develop a written and agreed upon marriage vision statement. It may start with just a couple of lines and then develop further, but vision is essential. Divine vision creates spiritual energy and it also releases pro-vision (for the vision). Most of the time when marriages are lacking provision it is because there is no vision. Nothing is required "for the vision." If you watch people's lives, those with the least amount of vision will have less provision than those with a vision. You will see the same patterns in business, ministry, and government. Even in our own country, as people have lost vision related to the nation America is supposed to be, we have lacked provision.

We wanted to share our personal marriage vision statement with you. It has developed over time, but from the beginning it has been an essential tool. We have to learn to do marriage INTENTIONALLY – it doesn't just happen! We hope that it will inspire you to begin work on your own statement. Even though we believe ours is a great one – don't just copy it. Work on developing your own. When we have reviewed other people's, they are all very personal and unique. Beginning a marriage vision statement is one of the things we have couples do at our marriage boot camps.

Our Marriage Vision Statement

We are called to have an example marriage for the Body of Christ and the world. God is first in our marriage and our marriage is our second priority after our relationship with Him. Our marriage is a healing place for ourselves and others. We are committed to staying physically healthy so we can enjoy each other, our family, ministry, and life. Our marriage is a place of adventure and never boring. It is an evangelistic and ministry tool. We continue to fall in love with each other on a daily basis. Our friends are motivated, young at heart, and support and appreciate our marriage. Our marriage is supernatural. We have strong boundaries and do not allow ourselves or others to bring strife, criticism, and inappropriate joking into our marriage. Our marriage is a refuge and safe place where we can be totally honest and fully ourselves. The anointing of God and His favor is upon every area of our marriage. Because we have a Kingdom Marriage, it is full of righteousness, peace, and joy.

When you review our vision statement, you can see that there is work and personal responsibility required from both parties. We can't cast off restraint and just get mad and stay mad if we are going to have an example marriage. It requires us to work through issues in order to be a safe place. It also makes us get out of bed several mornings a week to go to our exercise boot camp and eat a healthy diet so we can stay healthy. It helps govern and monitor relationships. It helps us set boundaries and priorities. I could go on and on, but you get the point. Our vision statement helped us set a course and also keeps us on course. It is something that needs to be reviewed, evaluated, and possibly added to on occasion. Where are we slipping? What do we need to adjust? Are we living up to the vision?

We can tell you that as couples begin to develop a vision statement – it is a unifying factor. It may take some work, but at least start. Even if you begin with one or two written lines, you can add to it. We started with one line, "We want our marriage to be an example marriage in the Body of Christ." One of the motivating factors for that beginning was that we saw so few truly healthy, happy, really functioning marriages. Many ministry marriages we were around were actually quite painful to observe. People can preach, move in the gifts, but still live in a miserable marriage. We had also worked with business people, some of them very wealthy, but still unsatisfied and in emotional pain because of their marriage relationship.

If you're going to have a Kingdom Marriage, it's going to take vision. We encourage you to begin to pray together and start writing down your Marriage Vision Statement. And when it's completed, if you have a family, take it one step further and develop a Family Vision Statement. Have some family meetings about it and then post it where it's visible to the whole family.

1. Do I understand God's vision for marriage?
2. What are some of the areas where my spouse and I have di-vision?
3. Do my spouse and I have an agreed upon vision for our marriage?
4. Do we have boundaries in our marriage?
5. What are some vision marriage elements that would be important to me?

CONCLUSION

We hope that through reading *Kingdom Marriage*, we were able to give you some practical as well as spiritual tools that can make a difference in your lives. We pray a blessing over your marriage and ask the Lord to bring healing and restoration over every damaged area. We pray for childish areas to mature and for truth to prevail. We pray that the Kingdom of God, righteousness, peace, and joy in the Holy Spirit would rule and reign in your marriage in the Name of Jesus.

God Bless You,
Rodney and Kathy Tolleson

FOR MORE INFORMATION ABOUT KINGDOM LIFE NOW:

KingdomLifeNow.com
Facebook.com/KingdomLifeNow1
Twitter.com/drkathytolleson

MORE BOOKS BY RODNEY & KATHY TOLLESON:
Kingdomlifenow.com/store

Restoring Sexuality
Soul Battles
Birth Assignments
Restore My Soul: 90 Day Devotional
Passivity: A Silent Killer
A Woman's Guide to Freedom
Prodigal Daughter
Redeemed
Staying Fresh